Monkey Bread Business

Leavensport, Ohio

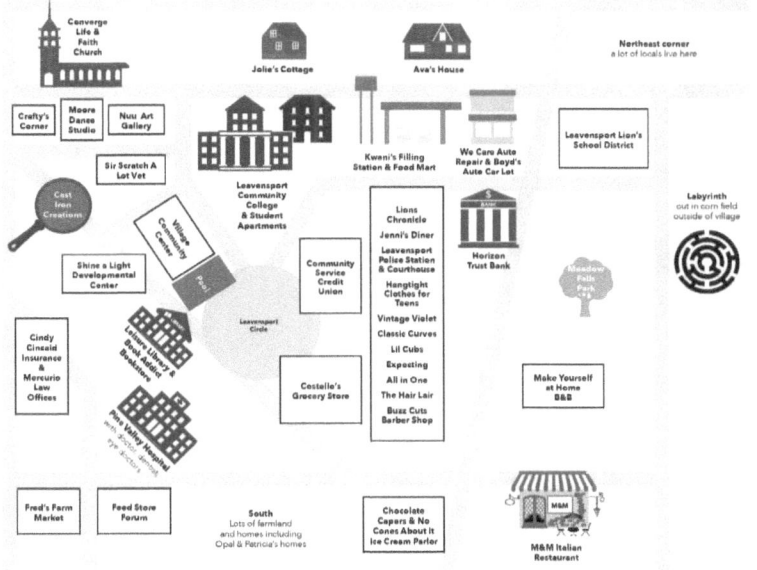

Monkey Bread Business

Book 6 in The Cast Iron Skillet Mystery Series

Jodi Rath

Copyright Page
Published by MYS ED LLC
PO Box 349
Carroll, OH 43112
jrath@columbus.rr.com

First Printing April 16, 2021
Copyright © Jodi Rath—MYS ED LLC, 2021
All Rights Reserved

Without limiting the rights under copyright reserved above, no part of this publication may be reproduced, stored in or introduced into a retrieval system, or transmitted, in any form, or by any means (electronic, mechanical, photocopying, recording, or otherwise), without the prior written permission of both the copyright owner and the above publisher of this book.

PUBLISHER'S NOTE

This is a work of fiction. Names, characters, places, and incidents either are the product of the author's imagination or are used fictitiously. Any resemblance to actual persons, living or dead, business establishments, events, or locales is entirely coincidental.

The publisher does not have any control over and does not assume any responsibility for author or third-party websites or their content.

The scanning, uploading, and distribution of this book via the internet or any other means without the publisher's permission are illegal and punishable by law. Please purchase only authorized electronic editions and do not participate in or encourage electronic piracy of copyrighted materials. Your support of the author's rights is appreciated.

https://www.jodirath.com

Note from the Publisher: The recipes contained in this book are to be followed precisely as written. Be aware that oven temperatures vary. The publisher and author are not responsible for your specific health or allergy needs that may require medical supervision. The publisher and author are not responsible for any adverse reactions to the recipes contained in this book or series.

Cover Design by Karen Phillips at Phillips Covers www.PhillipsCovers.com

Edited by Rebecca Grubb at Sterling Words www.sterlingwords.com

Formatted by Merry Bond at Anessa books anessabooks.com

Do we ever really know who our neighbors are?

~Earl Seevers

Dedication

Next month is Mother's Day. This book in the series is dedicated to my mom, Rosie Walton, who is my anchor. She was a single mom who gave me a passion for reading at a young age. She filled my room with Choose Your Own Adventure books and read them with me. She also subscribed to the Sesame Street Book Club and, every month, the morning my new book arrived felt like Christmas morning. We had a bookshelf filled with the worldly travels that I took from age four on.

One year, our local fair in Lancaster, Ohio had lots of cute giveaways for the tween girl that I was, but I wanted the set of Encyclopedia Britannica that was sitting among the other prizes. I signed up, and by gosh, I WON! We bought a special bookshelf for them, and, at seven years old, I used to play a game of closing my eyes and randomly picking a book then doing the same to pick an article in the encyclopedia. I'd voraciously read the article, take notes, and then write a summary of the article in my room, pretending I was writing for a magazine. And that is where my writing career really began—when I was that seven-year-old who turned to the world of books, reading, and stories to escape my world for but a time.

Thank you, Mom. You are my foundation. All of who I am comes from the foundation you laid for me, and I'll never be able to tell you in words how much I admire and love you!

Another mama to me is my mom-in-law, Dottie Rath, who passed away a while ago. Dottie took me into her family with open arms. She had the ability to make me smile every time I saw her beautiful face. She was the coolest ninety-something year old I've ever met in my life. I miss her daily but see her beautiful spirit in the amazing son she created.

Obviously, I can't write a dedication without mentioning the hubby and kitties—my entire heart, soul, and spirit! My besties—Rebecca, Rachel, Mary Ann, Leigh, and Kim.

Love to all the readers and to Missy Smith—girl, read the last section at the end of the book—more on you there!

I hope you all enjoy this book and have a fantastic upcoming Mom's Day!

The Leavensport Crew

Jolie Tucker—Co-owner of Cast Iron Creations, born in the village, best friend of Ava, granddaughter of Opal, daughter of Patty, married to Mick Meiser.

Ava Martinez—Co-owner of Cast Iron Creations, born in the village, best friend of Jolie, wife of Delilah, sister of Lolly, daughter of Sophia and Thiago.

Keith—Ex-boyfriend of Jolie, born in the village, best friend of Teddy—now, an officer of Leavensport.

Detective Mick Meiser—Jolie's new husband, from Tri-City, lives in Leavensport, owner of M&M's Italian Restaurant, police detective.

Maria—Mick's sister

Maya—Mick's mom

Chief Teddy Tobias—Police chief of Leavensport and born in the village, best friend of Keith.

Harvey Tobias—Teddy's dad.

Lydia—Jolie's frenemy, village nurse, best friend of Betsy, born in the village.

Betsy—Owns Chocolate Capers, best friend of Lydia, born in the village.

Bobby Zane—new principal of the Leavensport Lions High School

Delilah—Sister of Bradley, village artist, girlfriend of Ava.

Bradley—Brother of Delilah, village journalist.

Nina Sanchez—Mother of Luis and owns a new bakery in town.

Luis Sanchez—son of Nina, in high school.

Stella—Owns Ralph & Stella's New York Pizza.

Grandma Opal—Jolie's grandma, housewife who helped Jolie and Ava start Cast Iron Creations with her cast-iron skillet recipes.

Aunt Fern—Jolie's wacky, unpredictable aunt, sister to Patty, man-hungry.

Patty—Jolie's mom.

Mayor Nalini—mayor of Leavensport, Lahiri is his niece.

Jackson Nestle—Unscrupulous political associate of Mayor Cardinal from Tri-City

Caleb and Asher—works for Nestle's Construction Company

Lia—Nestle's ex-wife who is undercover

Devonte—knows who Lia is and protects her, works at shelter

Tom Costello—grocer in Leavensport; was engaged to Grandma Opal

Eddie—uncle to Jolie. Was estranged to family for decades with wife Shelly and five kids.

Wylie—uncle to Jolie.

Lory—Lydia's mom.

Karl—Lydia's dad.

Imelda—Italian princess

Tabitha—FBI and therapist of Jolie and Mick

Mary—Mirabelle's mom and Carlos' new wife

Carlos—Assistant manager at Cast Iron Creation, married to Mary, Mirabelle's step-dad.

Mirabelle and Spy—Young woman in her twenties with Down Syndrome with a seeing-eye dog, Spy.

Missy and Shelby Smith—Mother/daughter duo. Missy is running the Leavensport prom and Shelby is helping.

Chapter One

The last five months felt like a tornado had touched down right smack in the middle of my life. My wonderful new husband, Mick, and I bought a beautiful new home, but at the moment, it looked like it had been ransacked. Our belongings were scattered everywhere—boxes with clothes, dish rags, books, and cat toys overflowing. Mick was out in the garage setting up his man cave. I stood, hands on hips, looking up at the high ceiling of our living room before continuing my attempt to sort through it all.

Hopefully, he knows I can change the oil in my car myself, and that I'll be using those tools too! I thought to myself taking a seat on our oversized, comfy couch and reaching for the first exploding box I found near me.

Oh yeah, did I mention that living together meant we now had a total of eight cats? That equals seven stinky boys while Bobbi Jo, D.J., and I did our best to deal with the stench. To begin with, I was pretty sure I had the stomach virus going around town. All the boy odor was putting my gut even more on edge and having to hustle to the nearest bathroom to be sick every now and then wasn't helping me get things done. Plus, I was juggling co-running a restaurant and a part-time private investigation service, all with my BFF, Ava Martinez.

Over the holiday season, Ava married her soul mate, Delilah, and I spontaneously proposed to and married Mick during the double wedding ceremony. My grandma Opal and Tom Costello, Leavensport's local grocer, were supposed to be the other couple getting married that day, but my grandma found out some information from Tom's past and left him standing at the altar.

Grandma's ex-fiancé was more than a widowed local grocery owner. Grandma found out that back in the day when Tom's first wife was pregnant, his store was struggling. He had to borrow some funds to keep it afloat, and, in doing so, gained some not-so-desirable "influences" on his business decisions. He had to host illegal raves in the basement of his store for the Canadian mafia. Everywhere I turned, I realized someone had a dark secret. Skeletons weren't just falling out of closets—it seemed like they were raining down from the sky.

Yet, as stressed as I was, I had a lot more to be thankful for than not. I was thrilled that Mick and I had made it over the hurdles we'd been battling the last two years. Even though I knew life would continue to throw us curveballs, I had complete trust that he and I could work through anything that came our way. That was a HUGE hurdle for me personally, considering my past with men. Plus, I lived in a beautiful small village populated with many wonderful people. My family was, for the most part, supportive of my life, if maybe a tad too involved.

As much as I loved my family and my life growing up in Leavensport, I'd always been an odd duck—hiding in kitchens, walking around town with my earbuds in and a book in hand. I always carried a huge tote loaded with journals, books, music—an emergency kit that allowed me to disappear into my own world at any gathering that involved people. Yeppers, I was that gal.

Ava and I still hadn't debriefed one another on all the intel we'd gathered on historical town politics over the last few months. We desperately needed to meet for a full day to catch up on our I Spy Slides for our PI business that Ava titled Bounty-Full Investigative Services—*Food and Felony Fixes with Sass!* Hopefully, we'd never have to pay for a sign. We'd have to have a large building to fit that title.

"Earth to Jolie!" I jolted out of my reverie to find Ava snapping her fingers near my eyes. I sat up straight on the couch.

"Oh, when did you get here?" I shook my head to return fully to the present.

Ava's face was three shades of green, and her eyes bulged out as she looked around in a panic. She stood in front of me, wild curls frizzed out from the wind, her bag falling off her arm and a key in her hand. Behind her, my front door stood open as though she had burst through it in a rush.

"It's over there!" I pointed to the small guest bathroom located down the hall off the great room. Mick's head popped through the garage door just as Ava galloped down the hallway. She lunged for the bathroom door and slammed it behind her.

"Is she okay?" His face twisted in concern as he walked inside and closed the front door that she had left gaping open in her wild entrance.

"I hope she isn't catching what I have," I fretted, leaning away from him as he settled next to me on the couch. "You should stay away from us. There have been a ton of people in the village with this bug recently."

"It's going around the station, too. And Bea and Denise both had it last week, so we were short of help at the restaurant," Mick said, referring to his place, M&M's Italian Restaurant.

Like Ava and me, my hubby was an out-of-control multi-tasker—he was the only ranking detective in Leavensport and also a restaurant owner. He had MS and purchased the restaurant a couple of years ago to have if he got to the point with his health that he couldn't do police work any longer. Luckily, Teddy, the police chief, was a childhood friend and extremely understanding when Mick had MS flare-ups and needed to take extended periods of time off work.

"If half the town wasn't also sick in bed, I'd think it was that the three of us were burning the candles at both ends," I said, referring to how busy we all had been lately.

Ava came dragging back into the great room. "I used some of your mouthwash. Did you pass this thing on to me?"

"Who knows who is passing it around? You know how many people have had it," I said as Mick handed Ava a glass of water.

"Thanks." She guzzled it.

"Slow down there, champ," Mick said, reaching for the almost-empty glass.

"Sorry, Delilah's had this bug, too. I shouldn't have snapped at you, Jolie."

"It's okay. I haven't exactly been a beacon of joy

and sunshine either. Is Delilah okay?" I asked.

"She's been stuck at home for the last few days. I've been staying in the other room but trying to bring her soup and keep her hydrated. Anyway, not why I came today." Ava looked around the inside of our new home.

Things felt different now because Ava and I grew up as neighbors. When we got older, we bought cottages next door to each other. Then when Mick and I got married, he and I moved slightly out of town into an area that seemed to be out of range of future urban sprawl, for a while at least. This was the first time that Ava and I didn't live right next door and could pop over whenever. Granted, Ava and I were only a ten-minute drive apart, but it was still a big change for us. But it made for a great bike ride to and from our homes now. I still picked Ava up for work when we had the same shifts, which was most of the time. But I missed her barging in multiple times a day. I never thought I'd say that.

"Wow, this place is a mess," Ava said boorishly, looking around the open living room with the loft above. Then I saw her head swing in the direction of the open kitchen, my haven.

A long time ago, I found a spread in a magazine of a beautiful country kitchen done in old oak painted an antique green that had a vintage feel with grassy undertones. It reminded me of a granny smith apple. Later, when we were getting our new house ready, Mick had remembered me describing it and made a point to find that old edition of the *Better Homes and Gardens* magazine to make my dream kitchen come true.

There was a large bay window over the sink that overlooked our woods. The countertops were marble with a tannish hue that matched the light reds and pinks of the tile backsplash. The flooring was large tiles that matched those on the walls and had been laid individually by hand, showing the grayish clay grout in between each one. The tile led into the dining room that had a nook off towards the corner with a real, working antique cast-iron stove. The walls of the dining area were light gray stone with a white stucco ceiling supported by oak beams. A sliding glass door stood by the large oak table set we had in the middle and off to one side was a large bay window with a cushiony bench under it for reading—similar to the one we had recently added to Cast Iron Creations.

Ava strolled through the kitchen, looking around with an appreciative expression as she brushed her fingers along the marble counter and then moved to the dining room, feeling the stones of the wall, then sitting and looking out at the vista of blossoming crabapple trees. I loved the textures at work in this space and I could see she had noticed them too.

"I want to hold off organizing the kitchen until you have some time to come over and help me with it. Now, what did you come here to tell me?" I asked, tapping my foot.

"Oh, right, I'm not sure you should wait for me. I've got some serious investigating to do." Ava stopped talking and clutched her stomach, trying to squelch a belch as her cheeks bulged out.

"Do you need—" I started to move toward her but she got a determined look on her face and held a hand up firmly.

"I'm okay," she said, taking a deep breath and exhaling slowly. "I came here to tell you about the new bakery next to Mick's place. I just heard who bought it."

"Who?" I asked with a sinking feeling.

"Nina Sanchez." Ava gave me a meaningful look that I didn't understand.

I blinked several times. "Do I know her?"

"No. I don't either, but—" Ava started.

Then it clicked in my brain. "Sanchez!"

Suddenly visions of gold nuggets and pirate ships filled my mind, taking me back to the Dominican Republic when Ava and I visited her family.

"Yep, now do you see why we need to investigate?"

Chapter Two

The next morning, I was alone in the kitchen of the restaurant I co-owned with Ava, Cast Iron Creations, preparing some dishes for the day. I'd just finished making some of the standards for my morning regulars that would be coming in within the hour and getting a few things ready for lunch later. Next, I started a batch of cast iron monkey bread. I had experimented with the recipe in my new kitchen at home. Since I got started later than I anticipated due to a stomachache, I opted not to make these from scratch. I searched our large fridge and freezer, pushing fresh spring veggies and fruits to the side.

"YES!" I hissed to myself, lifting a knee and pumping an elbow as if tooting a train whistle after finding several canisters of store-bought biscuits.

As I opened the first canister, pulled the dough out, and sprinkled a bit of flour and a little pumpkin pie spice into the batter for a homemade kick, I thought back to the trip Ava and I took to Santo Domingo last year to help her family out of a jam. We'd uncovered two Latinx families that had a history of mafia activities—the Perezes and the

Sanchezes. Now, someone named Sanchez is opening a bakery here in Leavensport. Coincidence?

I began taking small chunks of the biscuit dough, dipping them into melted butter, then tossing them into a large plastic freezer bag, adding in granulated and brown sugar, cinnamon, and a bit more of the pumpkin pie spice. Then I closed the bag and shook the mix together.

The smell was amazing . . . at first—then my belly gurgled and I stepped back, putting a hand up to my nose and mouth. I took a deep breath and shook it off. This bug was not fun.

Well, I could take some of this monkey bread to Nina at her new bakery and discuss the cross-selling that we loved to do in the village so all of the businesses were supporting each other. Maybe Ava and I could find out a bit more about her past and where she came from—if it was the Dominican Republic, then chances were good she was a part of that family and that means she could be a part of smuggling things into our village for whatever reason these crooks seemed to be targeting our little town.

I laid the little balls of sweet and spicy dough next to each other in my large cast iron pan and placed them in the oven, then began whisking together the powdered sugar, cream, and vanilla in a separate bowl to get the drizzle ready to pour over the hot, buttery dough as soon as it came out of the oven. Regardless of how off my stomach was, my mouth still watered thinking about that drizzle taking form and hardening a bit on the dough and the flavors that would pop in my mouth when I tried a bite.

When I made it at home, Mick and I ate an

entire pan of it in one sitting. It was insane to think back to last year when I went away with Ava to get space from Mick to help me figure out how I felt about him. In a short amount of time—that really felt a lot longer—he and I figured out we were soul mates and we never wanted to be apart from each other again.

I smiled widely staring off into space thinking about Mick's dark, brown, soulful eyes—how he gave me a special look that I never saw him give anyone else and how my heart melted each time—

"Are you having a sex fantasy?"

I had been daydreaming while whisking the icing when Ava pulled me from my thoughts. I jumped, splattering icing onto Ava's terra-cotta skin.

"Sorry!" I squealed, giggling.

Ava wiped the icing off her cheek with a finger and plopped it in her mouth, then her dark eyes widened. "YUM!" She leaned over the bowl with that same finger sticking out.

I snatched the icing away. "Back off, woman. This is for the customers—don't contaminate it!"

"You're no fun!"

"Here's a tasting spoon." I gave her one and took one myself as we both swiped a little glop of the sticky drizzle and let it hit our tongues. We closed our eyes and moaned simultaneously.

"So, were you doing the nasty with your guy this morning or something?"

"First off, no. Second, that is none of your business—but yes, I was fantasizing about his eyes."

"You are SO boring! His eyes? I mean, I don't swing that way, but he does have a fine behind!"

"Why are you looking at my husband's butt? That's just rude!" I went to wash my hands and pushed a mesh of tight, dirty blonde curls away from my blue eyes.

We heard someone knocking in the front and both looked at our watches. It was three minutes past opening time and the regulars were gathered around the door for the takeout they always took to work. Ava ran up front as I got the meals I had prepared off the warmers and put them into takeout containers.

"You started the coffee pots, right?" I yelled up after Ava.

"Of course I did!" she yelled back. I heard her opening the door and saying to the customers, "Sorry about that, Jolie was holding me up—you know how chatty she can be."

I imagined her rolling her eyes as the regulars grinned to themselves, knowing I wasn't the chatty one of the pair.

"Hey everyone!" I said, carrying a pile of boxes up front to the counter. Magda had come in and ran to the back office for her apron and ordering pad for those that were taking seats. Ava got large to-go coffee cups and filled them, then counted out the sugars and creamers for those that would need them.

Missy Smith and her eight-year-old daughter, Shelby, were the first in line. The mother-daughter pair were both cute as buttons and like BFF's. "You both are busy—I need to ask you both something but it can wait."

Missy nodded at me, then paid as Shelby gave Ava a high five and they headed out to the Leavensport Lions school district for the day.

I yelled after them, "Just text me and I'll get back to you!"

She gave me a thumbs up as Bea and Earl Seevers came in and sat at their usual table. Things were hopping this morning.

A few hours later, business had calmed down and I checked my cell. Missy had texted asking if I would have time to meet her today or tomorrow. *I can take a break now. I'd love to take a walk. Want to meet me somewhere?* I messaged back.

I needed to fill Ava in on what had to be done in the kitchen while I was out with Missy. Ava seemed to be in a deep conversation with Bradley—once upon a time, he had been her beau…until she fell in love with his sister, Delilah. Luckily, everyone was able to work through the awkwardness and now the two were in-laws.

"Hey, Ava, I'm taking a break."

Ava's mouth continued to move, and she gave a half-nod in my direction.

"Ava, are you listening?"

Bradley looked from Ava to me, grinning uncomfortably as I gave him a preoccupied wave.

"There are enough biscuits left for eight more meals, then you'll have to prep more. Ava—" I huffed hugging my waist. "AVA!"

Ava continued to ignore my yells, nodded and waved a dismissive hand at me.

Fine. Have fun figuring all of that out while I'm gone.

Missy was waiting for me by Moore's Dance Studio, where she worked, and we walked through the village's art alley. I brought a cup of freshly made sweetened sun tea for each of us as we took a stroll, enjoying the sunshine, warmer air, and the fresh green leaves showing us that winter had passed.

"So, what's up?" I asked.

"Oh, it's not a big deal," Missy said, slurping some tea, "but as you know, I'm taking over prom duties this year with the new principal coming in last month."

"Uh-huh, what happened to Mr. Marlo anyway? As much as the gossip flies around here, I can't believe I've not heard the story."

"He retired and moved to be with his kids in Florida. His daughter is having his first grandchild and he's two years beyond retirement. He wanted to be there when the baby is born."

"Oh wow, well that's a great reason to leave early!" I exclaimed, realizing I had assumed that it was some ominous, dark reason and wondering if I'd been wrapped up in too many investigations the last couple of years. It was a breath of fresh air to hear some truly good news.

"Yeah, well, you know how new leaders love to change everything up. I do a lot of volunteer work at the high school with crafts and have helped in P.E. with some dance exercises—so, yeah, he decided he'd like a community member to take over this year's prom to get it promoted outside of the school and get the community more involved. I'm sure he has some future plans, but who knows? Anyhoo, would you be up for volunteering to chaperone? He asked me to recruit some prominent community members and you are one of the first people I thought of since you are a big part of the cross-selling among our local businesses." She bit her lip, looking like she thought I'd refuse on the spot.

"Of course. Put both me and Ava down. I'm not sure about Mick or Delilah, but I can wrangle Ava into it." I knew it would turn into an issue, but what didn't with Ava?

"Oh, that's great. I was hoping you'd volunteer to ask Ava." She giggled. "Mr. and Mrs. Seevers are going to chaperone too! Shelby asked them."

"I'm sure they couldn't say no to that sweet face."

"Who can?" She shrugged her shoulders as we circled back to the restaurant.

"Not me, and obviously, I can't say no to her mom either. Hey, you want some of our Cheesy Frittata with Spring Greens? I made some for brunch today. I can pack up a box for you on the house." I motioned for her to follow me into the restaurant.

"You know I'm never turning down free food." She followed me inside.

"Hey, Jolie," Magda said. "Ava had to go home. She was feeling under the weather. We didn't have many people in here so I told her I could handle it until you got back."

"Okay," I said, running back to pack a brunch box for Missy and carrying it back up. After Missy left, no one else was around, so I called Ava to check in.

"Do you need me to come back in?" Ava answered her cell with a question.

"Not if you're sick!" I exclaimed, thinking I may need to take my own advice if this bug didn't pass.

"I'm doing better. I could have stayed but I felt feverish for a bit and didn't want to risk passing anything to anyone."

Luckily, I wasn't experiencing that. "I made some extra monkey bread that I put aside. I'm going to run over to Nina Sanchez's bakery when Carlos comes in to take over the closing shift and see what I can find out."

"Stop and pick me up on your way," Ava said groggily.

"I'll text then to see how you are feeling."

"I just took some meds to help with the fever and I'm going to take a nap. I'll text you when I wake up and let you know."

Since there was a lull, I started prepping the dinner special for that night to save Carlos some time later. I pulled out the New York strip steaks I'd put in the fridge the night before and began patting them dry. I was adding some Kosher salt and cracked pepper to each side when there was a knock on the back door by the alley.

I washed my hands and ran to the back and cracked the door to see Lia standing outside, looking around. Lia's actual name is Natalia, who unfortunately used to be married to Jackson Nestle—the man Ava and I were positive was behind so much crime in our little hamlet the last few years. Natalia had changed her name to Lia when she went into witness protection after leaving Nestle.

"Hey, come on in," I said, taking a stool from the counter and dragging it back to the island where I continued working on the prep for my one-skillet steak dinner with spring veggies and Dijon glaze.

"That smells delish." Lia took a seat.

"Thanks, you hungry?"

"I don't turn down food." Lia smiled, referring

to when she skipped out on witness protection when she heard her ex, Nestle, was in Ohio, where her family is from, and took it upon herself to figure out that he was running the construction company that was building the new mall between Leavensport and Tri-City. She changed her name and her appearance, becoming unhoused and taking shelter in the tunnels that ran underground from Tri-City to Leavensport with a group of people that were also experiencing homelessness. Lia became a strong advocate for this group by the time she and I ran into each other in December. We worked together with the help of Mayor Nalini to get a shelter for unhoused residents in place between Tri-City and Leavensport. Yet another project that had kept me super busy since the holidays.

I grabbed a bowl and added some Thai chicken soup that was left over from last night's dinner and some homemade banana bread that Betsy made for cross-selling and popped it in the microwave.

As I put it in front of her, she asked, "You aren't having any?"

"Nah, I'm trying to fight off that stomach bug that seems to be going around town." I continued to whisk some mustard and vinegar in with the garlic I'd just minced and put a dash of cayenne into the mix, then picked up a tasting spoon to taste for flavor.

Lia almost spit her soup out laughing. "Your stomach hurts but you taste that. You are a true chef."

I grinned at the irony and shrugged. "So, what's up?"

"Last week, Jackson came to the shelter to drop off boxes with clothes, blankets, pillows, and food."

"What? Did he see you?" I asked, knowing that Lia put one of her friends in charge of running the shelter to keep her anonymity, but in actuality, she really ran the shelter.

"No, luckily, I was in the back warehouse and Devonte saw him first and texted me to stay there."

Devonte was one of the people Lia helped and he was extremely protective of her. He was the only other person besides me and Ava who knew who she really was.

"Why on earth would that man do anything nice?"

"There's something in it for him for sure. You better bet I personally went through every single box that he dropped off."

"Did you find anything?"

"Not a thing, but I lived with him—trust me, I know that man always has ulterior motives."

"I've never lived with him and I know that." We had a mutual animosity for Jackson Nestle.

Lia finished up her soup and pulled her wallet out of her purse.

I shook my head. "Nope, it's on the house today."

"Thanks so much! I wanted to let you know what was going on in case you wanted to keep track of it. I know you and Ava told me he's been up to no good with Delilah.

She was referring to Ava's wife, Delilah, who owned two businesses in the art district—one of which Nestle now owned a stake in after taking advantage of a bad situation last year.

Also—" Lia paused. "I'm going to do some more snooping. I'll be going back to being an unhoused resident to see if I can find out more about what those tunnels are actually used for."

"I don't like that idea at all. You've had too many close calls, not to mention you even living in this town puts you in danger."

"What you said is the exact reason why I need to do this. He's gotten away with way too much over the years. I know things that can bring him down but I need to get some proof to back it up."

"Can't you lay low while Ava and I find the time to sit down and review everything? We've been overwhelmed since the holidays with work, marriage, moving, and now we both are feeling under the weather. But let us handle this."

We both looked up as Carlos came in the front of the shop and headed to the kitchen.

"I hope you feel better soon. Thanks again for chatting with me." Lia got up and ducked back out the back as Carlos came through the swinging doors from the front.

I needed to find time to reach out to her before she did something that could put her life into more danger than it already was.

"You are prepping the steak special, I see," Carlos said, putting on his apron and washing his hands before taking over for the late afternoon and evening shift.

It was difficult for me to accept that he had purchased some land and had plans to open a Mexican restaurant this summer. We were going to have to find a new chef for our little joint and I was going to miss him terribly.

"Yep, we were really busy when we opened this morning right into the lunch hour but then we hit a lull this afternoon. I don't know what that means for you tonight," I said, grinning at his Garfield tee that showed the orange tabby wolfing down a whole lasagna in one bite.

"I'm positive it's busy tonight. Everyone loves the steak special. Thank you for starting it. I take over from here, though."

Man, Carlos loved to cook as much as I did. We had quickly bumped him to an assistant manager as soon as we had the funds. He worked harder than we did half the time and took such pride in his work. I was thrilled for the opportunity for him to open his own place, but I was equally saddened too.

"How are Mary and Mirabelle doing?" His now wife, Mary, was the mother of Mirabelle, our hostess with the mostess, a twenty-something woman with Down Syndrome who always had her sidekick Spy, a cocker spaniel, to help her with her sight.

"They are good. Mary will be due with our son soon." Carlos' smile brightened the entire room.

"I know. You know you can take whatever time off you need when the baby comes right?"

"Hello?" we heard someone call out.

"Speak of the devil," I said looking up to see Mary waddle through the swinging doors.

Carlos ran around the island to help her to a chair he pulled out of the office which she waved away. "She no devil, she my angel."

"She was kidding Carlos—remember, we talked about American idioms? I need to stand and stretch my legs. I've been cooped up too long and Delilah came to take Mirabelle to do some crafts so I thought I'd drop by before running over to pick her up." She reached down and rubbed her belly and had a distraught look on her face.

"Are you okay?" I asked moving to rub her arm in concern.

"Yeah, sometimes I wonder if I'm not catching that bug that's going around or if it's this baby boy inside me begging to get out."

"Ah, see, cooped up is idiom, yes?" Carlos asked Mary.

Mary had an odd look on her face. "Yep, I didn't think you'd be here so early."

That seemed odd she'd say that. I assumed she stopped in to see him. Mary looked around awkwardly and I shrugged it off to pregnancy hormones and headed out.

I ran a file over to Tabitha, who was Mick's and my therapist, slipping it in her mailbox in the lobby of her office. Mick had asked me to drop it off before I came home. I'm sure it was police business but was very proud of myself that I resisted snooping. Tabitha worked with the small police department in town since she had FBI experience.

With Mick's MS constantly in flux, he planned to continue seeing Tabitha as a therapist from time to time to help him cope with the emotional roller coaster it took him on—I also planned to see her on my own but less often.

Ava had texted me a few minutes ago that she felt a lot better and wanted me to pick her up on the way to Nina's bakery.

I pulled into the drive at Ava's and PopTart, their schnauzer, came scuttling up, barking as I got out of the car. "Hey, girl, how you doing? Are those little black kitties torturing you and you needed a break?" I bent down, scratching her chin as her little ears perked up.

Delilah and Ava came out and I saw three curious faces peer out the front window. Ava had adopted three little five-week-old black kittens last year and they were growing up fast. Lily, Luna, and Lulu were pistols just like their mama, Ava, was.

"Poppy, are you begging for love?" Delilah asked as the little chocolate brown furball ran on its short little legs to her.

"You'd think we never paid you any attention," Ava said, rubbing her behind her ears after Delilah picked her up.

"You two stay out of trouble." Delilah waved as she took the pup inside.

"She knows us so well." I looked behind me as I pulled out of the drive. I glanced over at my old cottage with sorrow. I had put my house up for sale and got an immediate buyer. I knew that people would be moving into town with the mall and business expansions. I was floored when I went to the closing to see Marissa from Deep Dish Done Right was the new owner.

"You miss it?" Ava asked.

I stopped the car at the end of the drive and cocked my head toward her. "Not really. I miss that it was the first thing to call mine after we opened the restaurant together and had enough income to buy houses."

"You miss *me*, though. There's NO way you don't miss *me*." Ava stuck her chin out at me.

"THAT has been the biggest blessing since I moved—the peace—the quiet—the—OW!" I yelled as Ava slugged my arm a little too hard.

I drove past the farm market and Costello's grocery toward the area beyond Mick's Italian restaurant, M&M's, and pulled into the little bakery called Pastry Spree's parking lot with only six spaces.

"Cute name," I said as I got out and popped the trunk to pull out the monkey bread as a peace offering to compensate for the grilling Nina was about to get.

As Ava and I walked into the shop we heard a greeting, "Hola," that came from a perky voice from a short, stocky woman who wore jeans with tennis shoes and a light-yellow sweater that had a chartreuse colored apron over it that said *Where There's a Whisk, There's a Way* and a cartoon cupcake that said "Pastry Spree" on the wrapper.

"Hi, wow, what a cute place!" I exclaimed, taking it all in. It was a tiny building with a peach-and-white tiled floor, a matching small counter. A display filled with all kinds of baked concoctions filled my vision as I felt my stomach rumble.

"How can we help you today?" The lady who I assumed to be Nina asked.

"Well, I'm Jolie and this is Ava—we co-own Cast Iron Creations and we brought you some monkey bread as a welcome gift." I smiled and handed her the Tupperware full of doughy goodness.

"How wonderful," she said, reaching for it and then shaking our hands.

A young boy came out from the back with a backpack on and a scowl on his narrow features. He looked to be in the middle of a heated conversation. "Yeah, well, I don't care. He's new too. What a militant jerk!"

"Luis!" Nina scolded the teen.

"Gotta go." He hung up and put his cell in his

back pocket. "Sorry, Mama."

"Please, these nice ladies brought us a gift to welcome us to town and you with your manners."

Ava and I looked at each other and smiled a little. I was not sure what to say.

"Hello, I'm Luis Sanchez." The boy politely reached for our hands to shake them. "I apologize for my behavior," he said, bowing slightly.

"No problem. Ava is like that all the time." I flicked my thumb towards her, giving Luis a knowing glance.

"Another new student at school?" Ava asked Luis while gently shoving me for my comment.

"Nah, the new principal. I didn't know the old one, but everyone seemed to like him a lot better than this guy." Luis turned and bent down to kiss his mom, said it was nice meeting us, and took off out the door.

Nina raised a hand and waved it after her son, "Ah, teen boys, what does one do with them? Come, ladies sit, please, I'll get us some coffee, yes?"

"I'll have some," Ava said, while I passed and opted for a glass of water but also took a triple chocolate cupcake.

"Sanchez was the last name?" Ava asked.

"Yes," Nina said, biting into a piece of pie she had sliced for herself.

"My last name is Martinez. My family is from Santo Domingo. There are Sanchezes there too. I don't suppose you're any relation?"

Whoa, I guess Ava wasn't going to beat around the bush.

Nina got an odd look on her face. "Hm, no, not us. I've never heard of them."

Silence. I think Ava hoped Nina would offer up more information, but she didn't seem keen on doing so.

"Well, one of the things we wanted to throw out to you was that many of the small businesses here in the village do something called cross-selling. We try to help each other out by sharing what we make with each other so when we get customers, hopefully we can get people to try other places too. The hope is that it benefits all the businesses."

"Oh, yes? Does it cost to belong to this?" Nina speculated.

"No, not at all," I replied. "Each person who participates keeps a pamphlet holder by their register or a bulletin board up with business cards and information about the other businesses. You don't have to participate if you don't want or you can wait awhile to decide if it's right for you or not."

"I will definitely give it some thought," Nina said. "Thank you for offering."

We got up to leave and I pulled out my wallet to pay for our cupcakes and drinks.

"That will be fourteen dollars and fifty cents." Nina rang up the small coffee, water, and two cupcakes.

I managed to prevent my jaw from dropping to the floor, but Ava didn't fare so well.

"For that?" Ava gulped.

I elbowed her and she looked at me like *what the?*

Nina held her ground in silence, staring at Ava. I noticed there was no pricing yet up on the large board with items for sale. I handed her a twenty, noting to myself I'd be frequenting Betsy's place more often than here. While the cupcakes were delicious, seven dollars apiece was steep, at least in these parts of Ohio.

"So, are you from the Dominican Republic?" Ava asked as Nina pulled change out of the register.

Nina stared silently at Ava with an odd smile on her face. I felt very uncomfortable and thanked her, told her it was nice meeting her, and we took off.

Chapter Three

"She's an odd duck," I said as we pulled out of the parking lot.

"She's lying through her teeth," Ava harrumphed.

"Ready for the Manic Monday Monthly Meeting?" I changed the subject with Ava as we drove from Pastry Spree to the Leavensport Community Center.

"As much as anyone can be ready for these," Ava said.

Our village had monthly meetings to discuss news with town businesses, future projects, and many times, gossip came up as well. We always had lots of food, which was the highlight of the event. The community center had a cafeteria-type room in it for gatherings and a large theater-type room for performances. Mayor Nalini wanted the meetings to be held in the theater so he could take center stage and have all eyes on him, except he didn't want food in the theater—so, since no one obeyed the rules, we now had it in the cafeteria and he had to settle for standing at the side of the large room to lead the meetings. This, of course, was all suggested by my Aunt Fern who had been dating Mayor Nalini on and off for some time now.

"What did you bring as food tonight?" Ava asked.

"I made six deep-dish pizzas. They're in the warmers in the trunk." Those had been selling like crazy since last fall.

"Can't go wrong with pizza. That sounds delicious. I could eat two of them myself." Ava reached in her purse and pulled out a large dill pickle.

"What on earth?"

"It's a pickle in a pouch," Ava said, tearing open the plastic and taking a huge bite, groaning in delight.

"PEEW!" I swiped my hand in front of my nose. "That stinks! Roll your window down," I said, pressing the button to open the sunroof in my Honda Accord.

"Don't be such a baby. Geesh," Ava said as she pulled an Almond Joy out of her bag, ripping it open with her teeth and then taking alternating bites of pickle and candy bar.

I gagged and turned my head toward the driver's side window. "What in the heck are you doing?"

"Having a snack. I've been sick. I'm finally hungry now!"

We pulled into the full parking lot toward the back. "Do you want me to drop you off up front?"

"That's nice, yes," Ava said, taking another bite of each.

I pulled up front and let Ava out after she wolfed down the last of her pickle and candy bar.

She grabbed a few pizzas from the back. "Braaadley!" Ava yelled, waving her arms. I saw him grin, shake his head, and saunter over. She got him to take the other warmer with the remainder of the pizzas. I waved at him before going to park in the back. I decided to let all four windows stay cracked to air out the nutty sour smell that reeked within my car.

I was thinking about tonight's agenda, which dealt with the plans for the new mall, as I was walking into the center. Ava and I made up the name Manic Monday Meetings because Mondays were always so crazy and our town meetings tended to be a bit eccentric. When you pulled in a lot of locals who were born and raised in the town where their ancestors lived, everyone had strong opinions and weren't shy about sharing. It often led to colorful language and at times got a little too intense. You never knew what to expect.

Walking into the kitchen, I started pulling pizzas out and got a plate to take a slice for myself. I was feeling better and realized I was famished. I took a big bite and moaned loudly. Wow, I was an amazing chef if I said so myself—which I did.

"Oh, wow, I was just coming to get these to put out front."

I looked up to see Marissa, the woman who had recently moved to our town and actually purchased my first home. She had also recently opened Deep Dish Pizza Done Right. She was walking next to her new full-time help, Roxi who smiled awkwardly at me.

"Huh?" I said unintelligently.

"The pizzas." Marissa pointed to what I was eating.

"These are yours?" I asked incredulously. They tasted exactly like mine and the warmers looked like mine too.

"Jolie, you totally outdid yourself—these pizzas are amazing!" Ava walked up with a plate that was piled with six huge pieces of the saucy, cheesy concoction.

"Where'd you get that?" I asked, my eyes traveling back and forth between her plate and the pizza on the table.

"Out front. Bradley and I just put the pizzas out. Whoa, you brought more?"

"No, these are my pizzas," Marissa huffed, crossing her arms.

"Let me taste." Ava reached over and served herself a seventh piece of pizza and took a huge bite. Her eyes widened. "This tastes EXACTLY like ours. What the—"

"Sorry," I interrupted, knowing this wasn't going to be pretty, "but you made these and these are your warmers?"

I looked under the flap to see if my sticker *This warmer belongs to Jolie Tucker!* was there. Nope. I looked to Ava and shook my head.

"Yes, this is my recipe and my warmer bags. Now, if you'll excuse us, we need to get set up." Marissa and Roxi pushed past us with their bags of identical pizza.

I curled my lip and dropped the half-eaten slice of Marissa's imposter pizza into the trash.

"You're going to be THAT girl," Ava said, then added, "I approve."

"I don't like her and I think it's weird that Roxi is working with her. Also, you tasted it! It tastes exactly like ours. I mean EXACTLY!" I was beyond worked up over this for some reason.

"If it isn't my two favorite gals!" Stella walked up, smiling. She was the new owner of Ralph's pizza place which was now named Ralph & Stella's New York Pizza.

"Do you know Marissa from the new deep dish pizza place in town?" Ava asked.

"Sure do, she visited my shop to try out some competition," Stella said, wiggling her eyebrows.

"Have I shared my deep-dish pizza recipe with you?" I asked in a more accusatory voice than I meant to. "You didn't share it with her, did you?"

Stella looked crestfallen. "Um—no—no, I don't think you ever shared it. But if you did, I'd never do something like that to you, Jolie."

Even Ava was taken aback by my rude behavior as tears welled up in Stella's eyes. Great, she had enough trouble with some jerks in society who harassed her for being trans, now I went and added myself to the jerk list.

"I'm so sorry. I don't know what's wrong with me. My moods have been insane lately—not that that's an excuse for talking to you that way."

"It's okay. I have my days too." Stella looked down at her hands.

"Seriously, don't pay any attention to Grumpy McGrumperson here—she was all over me about my snacks in her car. I just ignore her when she gets like that," Ava said, making me momentarily want to elbow her until I realized Stella needed someone to back her up after my bad behavior.

My entire body must have slumped because Stella looked like she felt for me. *Great, not only was I a jerk, but I was a feel-bad-for-me-for-being-a-jerk jerk!* "I feel like there is no good way for me to apologize. Behaving that way with Ava is one thing, you are a whole different story!"

I reached out to hug her and she graciously squeezed me back. "I'll take it as a compliment that you love me as much as this one." She jerked her thumb toward Ava.

I smiled. "Please do."

Mayor Nalini banged a gavel on a cafeteria table loudly signaling the start of the meeting. The loud mumbling lowered to barely a whisper as everyone took a seat and started chowing down.

I looked through the agenda that had been emailed out this morning as the mayor begin moving through the points. I took a big bite of my deep dish, but I was so frustrated at how Marissa's "signature" deep dish tasted exactly like mine that I couldn't enjoy it—so I shoved it away.

Grandma Opal was sitting across from me and glanced skeptically in my direction, then shrugged. She took the two pieces off my plate onto hers, making it heap into a large tower of deep-dish delight.

The mayor seemed to be going through the list of topics quickly, explaining some new businesses to open soon in our village from the farmland that's been sold. Whispering mumbles turned to grumbles—no one in the village was in favor of expansion into the city. Yet Carlos would get his opportunity at the American dream with this development, so it couldn't be all bad—except for the mysterious criminals who were extorting him.

Ava, who was sitting on my right, side-kicked my calf under the cafeteria table and I yelped out loud, then covered my mouth quickly as all eyes turned to me. My hubby, on my left, leaned into my ear with a smirk on his face. "You're up, sweetie."

I looked quizzically at him, then realized where the mayor was on the list—he'd just announced the new Tri-City/Leavensport mall had an opening date of Spring of 2023 and the use of the "recently discovered" underground tunnels between the city and our town would be put to good use by the Nestle Construction Company. I had to give the monthly update on cross-selling and make our little hamlet look the appropriate part.

"Sorry." I glared at Ava as I stood with my journal full of my notes in hand. "We've added a few of the newer businesses to our cross-selling promotions and—" I put both hands over my stomach as it gurgled loudly. I noticed Grandma Opal, Aunt Fern, Uncle Wylie, and my mom sitting across from me, staring straight at my stomach. That answered that—others heard that too.

My mouth went from dry to watery in seconds as I felt the chunks of saucy pizza I just ate start to come back up. I slammed the chair behind me to the floor and sprinted down the hall toward the bathroom and was *so* close to making it. I yanked on the bathroom door. Locked. I fell to my knees and disaster spewed out. I had almost made it.

The door slowly opened, and Marissa stood with a slathering of freckles across her nose and long, loose, icy-white-blonde curls that swirled down to near her waist. Her one eye color was green while the other was dark hazel, making her look rebellious yet sophisticated. She was staring down at me with an odd grin on her face. I looked up, wiping my mouth as she held her hands up in the air over her head. "Hey, I'm sorry, I didn't know you were sick." She took a huge step over my mess and added, "I noticed you ate *your* pizza last, too."

Without thought, as she stated her comment her front leg was lifted over my mess, I grabbed hold of it as she went SPLAT and slipped through my barf.

Foul language rang throughout the hall as many left their tables trying to get a glimpse of what had happened in the hallway. "YOU—" Marissa stopped suddenly, then her facial expression shifted from wretched anger to sullenly hurt.

"Why would you do this to me? What did I ever do to you?" Marissa's facial expression and tone changed on a dime when she saw she had an audience, hiding her true colors.

"Jolie, come on—" Keith started jogging down the hall to help Marissa. "Are you okay?"

"Yes, I was trying to get past her to go get some towels to get her cleaned up when she reached for my leg, dragging me down." Marissa looked down at me, shaking her head and looking sad.

I knelt, my hands on the dirty floor, still swallowing hard from the queasiness I felt. I couldn't believe how she changed so quickly and lied so blatantly.

"What is your problem?" I managed to spit out as I began to stand to do a walk of shame.

"Jolie, I'm sorry I was in the bathroom when you needed it but—"

"Don't bother, Marissa—Jolie, grow up. Seriously," Keith stated, helping Marissa down the hall as Ava, my family, and hubby came toward me with clean-up gear in hands.

"What was that all about?" Ava asked as she stood erect, turning her head to one side and putting her hand to her nose.

"She's insane. You shouldn't be here or you'll

be sick too," I said.

"She's right—listen to Jolie. Mick, you get those two girls home and we'll get this cleaned up," Grandma Opal said, reaching for Uncle Wylie to help her to her knees to start cleaning. I guess once a mom, always a mom! Grandma didn't seem phased by it.

Delilah swept in and grabbed Ava and Mick helped me to the truck. Ava was going to drive my Honda back to our house and Delilah would follow. We were all climbing into the vehicles when Mary came hollering after us.

"Girls, I can't run that fast right now!"

We turned around to see Mary holding her protruding baby belly, trying to run.

"Whoa, slow down!" Ava said, hands out as if the baby would fall out of her.

"Okay, no—I'm good," Mary was panting, trying to lean over, but her baby bump was getting too big.

That little guy was coming soon or Mary was going to pop!

"Whoo, Jolie, Ava." Mary looked to Mick and Delilah awkwardly.

"Oh yeah, we'll go get the cars ready," Delilah said, turning my husband, who was clueless, around to give us some privacy.

"Are you okay?" I reached for her but saw her repulsed by my smell. "Sorry." I pulled back.

"No, I'm sorry. You need to go home and rest. I wanted to talk to you both when Carlos or Mirabelle wasn't around. Um—" She fiddled with her hands, then reached up to wipe a tear from her eye. "—I think he's in real trouble—Carlos."

"So, you know?" Ava asked, rubbing her arm.

"Ye—Yes, YOU BOTH KNOW!?" she yelled-slash-cried simultaneously.

"We don't know all the details. It's a long story, but he didn't do anything wrong. We can all sit down and discuss it, but I'm so sorry I have got to get home and get a shower." I felt bad bailing on her but the smell of me was making me worried I'd do a repeat performance.

"Of course, just—I think his family in Mexico is being threatened. I'm not sure, but there are things I've seen and overheard."

"You go, Jolie. I'll stay with Mary," Ava said. I nodded and I walked off hesitantly. *Dang this stupid stomach flu bug!*

Last night, I went straight home, showered, and fell asleep for a solid twelve hours. I woke refreshed and was happy I felt so much better. I had today off and needed to get ready to spend some time with Mick's mom and sister. We were having a "girls' day out to get to know each other better per his sister. I hoped today went better than previous encounters with Mick's family.

"Feeling better, sicky?" Mick asked, stepping out of our large, shared bathroom with a shower, a tub, and a small hot tub off in the corner. He had a towel around his waist and was glistening with water as steam poured from the bathroom. I felt like I was inside a Danielle Steele novel waiting to be taken by this hunk of man meat.

I pulled myself out of my romantic fantasy. "SO much better! I hope today goes well." I threw the covers off, forgetting poor Lenny and Bobbi Jo were snuggled up sleeping next to each other. They both hissed and ran out of the room.

"Sorry guys!" I yelled after them, watching Mick shake his head in disapproval. "What, I was preoccupied thinking about—" I felt my cheeks flush and got up, moving past him to find my jeans and a sweatshirt.

Mick grabbed me and pulled me to him, bending his body down to meet my forehead with his. I rubbed his muscular arms and grinned. "—nothing, there's not time for that now. Your family already can't stand me because they weren't at the wedding. Not that they were impressed before that."

"Who cares what they think? They're criminals," Mick said through gritted teeth.

I still couldn't understand how he could be so cold toward his family. I mean, my family made me INSANE on the daily, but still, I loved them. If they were in trouble, I'd drop everything to be there. I'd had this conversation before and his reply was always the same—my family is not a bunch of criminals. True. But still . . .

I kissed Mick on the way out. "Wish me luck."

"Just be you. They can like you or not. If they are rude, just leave or call me. I'll come get you. You know I don't expect you to try with them, right?"

"I know, but it seems they are making more of an effort with you and I want you to have your family too." I rubbed his arm.

"You and our cats are my family. That's all the family I need. Family comes in different forms. Not everyone has a traditional family."

I slid my hand from his bicep to his hands and squeezed them. "You know you are a part of the Tucker family whether you want to be or not." We both grinned. "But you're right. We are a family and we are all enough for each other."

I got to our little Leavensport mall at exactly eleven a.m. for our lunch. I would have been a bit early except Mick kept me at home a little longer than I expected—not that I was complaining.

Maya and Maria already had a seat at Jenni's Diner with coffees in front of them.

"Hello, sorry I'm a little late—" I started.

"We figured you'd be a little late, dear," Mick's mom, Maya, said, taking a well-manicured hand to pour her creamer in her coffee.

I noticed she had Jenni bring a silver creamer as she was not using the plastic ones from the booth.

"Why do you say that?" I couldn't help but ask.

"Oh, you know, small town people tend to go at a slower pace. Seems like you may need to change your rhythm soon enough as this little village of yours will be hopping within a few years."

"Mother, be nice," Maria said, rolling her large dark eyes at me.

"Nah, she's fine and partially right. We do work at our own pace here. But small-town folk keep big-city slickers in business with the produce from the farms, not to mention places to get away from the fray and so many more benefits when it comes to rural living. That and our lifestyle is more environmentally friendly most of the time too!" I smiled graciously as I waved for Jenni to bring me a glass of sweet tea.

Maria's phone rang and she looked down. "I need to take this." She got up and moved to the counter.

Maya looked around and sighed, then flipped

her thick, long, straight locks dramatically. "Excuse me dear, I need to find a suitable restroom."

With that, she got up and left the diner. My mouth dropped open and like the big baby I was, tears started to form. Why was I feeling guilty? She was the one who was rude to me in that manipulative way women can be where they "pretend" with their tone to be nice, while their eyes and the crocodile smile let you know exactly where you stand.

I took a few deep breaths and smiled up at Jenni as she delivered my iced tea. "Hang in there. They haven't been pleasant to me either, and they keep turning their noses up to every person who walks inside."

I started to apologize for my in-law's behavior, but Jenni saw it coming and held up a hand. "Not up to you to apologize for overly privileged snobs. Lord knows they'll never apologize. I figure I'm happy and they are obviously miserable and make a choice to be so. You do you, hon," she said with a smile and a wink.

Boy, now I was getting teary-eyed for a whole different reason. I didn't feel sick anymore—why were my moods on such a rollercoaster ride?

I sat looking at the emails on my phone and noting that Ava texted me blabber five times, my mom texted to remind me to wear my mouth guard at night. She thought my headaches lately could be due to me trying to show off for my new "beau" as she calls Mick. Grandma Opal texted to tell me she noticed my roots were getting straight when I was on the floor sick last night and I really should think about scheduling an appointment to get a perm. Phone off.

I looked up at Maria who was now leaning back

casually on the stool at the counter. I didn't think she even realized her mother had up and left. She nodded and furrowed her brow while talking to whomever it was. "Sure, it's not a problem to get that shipped to Ohio at all."

A long lull of silence, then, "No—no, seriously, don't worry about the cost. Our family will absorb the cost to get the materials here."

Okay, I was feeling bad I'd heard some stuff until that. I slid to the edge of my side of the booth, one butt cheek hanging off, trying to hear more. I understood why Mick struggled with his family. They were a mafia family. He changed his name and walked away from them to follow a career in law enforcement. Still, though, family. Ugh, he was right, I couldn't relate to his situation. My family was just a helicopter family and I wanted to disown them fifty percent of the time. I'd be done if they were a mafia family.

I reached for my tote, put my phone in it, and picked up my keys to head out. I threw down a twenty-dollar bill to compensate Jenni for having to put up with the Milano family.

"Where are you going?" Maya followed after me as I opened the diner door to leave.

"Oh, I thought you left and Maria was on the phone so I decided—"

"You always run off if you don't get your way?" Maya asked, crossing her arms and glaring at me.

My brain went momentarily numb. Was she blatantly baiting me? I watched her narrow-toed Manolo Blahnik's tap impatiently on the concrete in time with her blood-red manicured nails tapping her arm.

"Where did you two run off to and who left a

twenty for three cups of coffee?" Maria asked, walking up to us, swirling her expensive-looking fur over her shoulders.

"I guess the new Mrs. Milano feels like she's married into money so she can fling around a twenty for cheap, watered-down coffee," Maya sneered, staring me down.

I felt a mixture of anger, embarrassment, sadness, and hilarity. Yes, hilarity too. This situation seemed unreal to me.

"Mother!" Maria screamed.

"Who were you talking to anyway?" Maya asked.

"I heard you talking about shipping something here. A product of some sort. Can I help with something?" I couldn't help but ask.

"Why were you listening to my conversation?" Maria was quick to jump fences to her mom's side.

Now I crossed my arms. "I was sitting in a booth right next to you. Your mom walked out. You weren't exactly whispering."

Maria had that whole sweet-slash-hate façade going just like her mother. She gave me a look that could have killed me then switched to that same crocodile smile with all that fake sweetener. "You know, I've told that brother of mine he really needs to switch to using the family extra virgin olive oil. I mean, that restaurant has our name, after all. It makes sense to use the family oil from Sicily."

"It's M&M's for Mick Meiser. Not Mick Milano." I stuck my chin out, then immediately felt like a rat fink for saying something so horrible. No reason for me to sink to their level—but, too late.

Maria pretended not to hear me. I felt my emotions stirring more and more and was trying to take deep breaths without them noticing how much they were getting to me.

"Has Mick ever made Pasta alla Norma for you with our family's oil? It's a huge staple in Sicily."

I shook my head.

"I'll make some for you. Then, you can appreciate the taste of real olive oil and what it does to a dish." She punctuated this statement with a chef's kiss, then shook her head as though someone like me could never fully understand what she was talking about.

"So, who *were* you talking to?" Maya sharply emphasized each new syllable to her daughter.

Maya grinned evilly at her mother. "Imelda."

"Ahhh, Mick's long-lost love. I love luxurious perfumes but Imelda, that Alaïa Paris she wears..." Maria put her index finger and her thumb together and drew an imaginary line in the air like she was pulling closed a zip signaling perfection like the Italian gesture. Then she said, "*Perfetto*, and how is the ever-so-beautiful Sicilian princess doing?"

"The what now?" I said dully.

"Oh, those two, so much love. If only—" Maya looked to a faraway land.

"She asked about him—and you," Maria said nodding toward me. "Don't forget about the Balmain Paris headbands. That leather. Even makes us Italians jealous."

I ignored the info on how stylish Mick's long-lost love was and asked, "Me? I've never even heard of her."

"Well, she's heard of you, my dear. Trust me." Maya narrowed her eyes at me. "She wants to know you since you married my Mick."

I felt blood red heat flush up from my neck to my cheeks. Anger and tears started to well up within me. Mick was right. These people were horrible.

I turned away and stomped toward my car. I heard both of them make whimpering pleas for me to come back. Fake pleas. They were trying to save face at this point. I didn't care. I just didn't want to let them see me cry. Tears began spilling down my cheeks as I turned the corner of the sidewalk to where I parked in the mall parking lot.

I saw Keith's sister, Denise, outside of Hang Tight Clothes for Teens, she was waving her shopping-bag-laden arms around, facing another figure whose face I couldn't see. As I got closer, I heard her yelling, "You aren't so perfect yourself. No one knows all of the crap you've been involved in over the years. Don't you dare threaten me, Darrell! I could have you put in jail!"

I stopped in my tracks, debating whether to turn around and go back toward the mean Milano girls or have to pass this to get to my car. I looked both ways, then noticed Darrell and Denise looking at me. I waved lamely.

"Sorry, I was just walking to my car. I didn't mean to—"

"Don't apologize, Jolie. Darrell was just leaving." Denise glared at him.

Darrell, Denise's now ex-husband, scowled at me, then at Denise, and turned around, jogging away.

"Are you okay?" Denise asked me even though she was the one who needed a shoulder to lean on now.

"I'm just fed up with some stuff," I said. "Looks

like you can relate."

"Uh yeah. And I don't mean to be rude, but I need to pick the kids up and I need a little quiet time before I do."

"Say no more. I'm a girl who understands the need for peace and quiet," I said as we parted ways.

My mind wandered with thoughts of how difficult family could be as I drove home. I pulled into the drive and took a breath. Mick's truck was in the driveway. I was hoping he had to work late so I could get my bearings.

I hefted my large tote onto my shoulder and headed inside to a warm welcome from some furballs. "Hi babies," I squealed and bent down to nudge ears, pat their behinds, and do a quick pick up for head kisses.

I threw my body on the couch and reached for my laptop, searching for Alaïa perfume and my mouth dropped. There were only three hundred made in the world and it cost twenty-five hundred dollars for one ounce. I started crying again. Why was I so emotional?

"Hey babe, I brought some pizzas home from the restaurant. I didn't think about you getting sick on it last night until it was—whoa, what's wrong? What did they do?"

"What?" I looked at him innocently.

"Don't even—your mascara is running down your cheeks. Your face is pale and you can't hide a thing with your eyes. I can see the pain in them. What did they do? Tell me now." Mick's neck was beginning to flush red and he clenched his jaw.

"Thanks for being so protective. Seriously, I don't think it's as bad as I'm making it look. I don't think I felt as good as I thought and my emotions have been all over the place today. AND, don't you dare ask me if it's that time of the month, mister!" I scolded playfully, trying to change the topic.

I thought about asking him about Imelda, but I figured that may create more interrogation of what all was said today and I didn't want to get into all of it. I was saved by the bell.

"Your butt dung," I said.

"What?" Mick said.

"Your butt—it is dinging—it dung," I said, pointing to his pocket. "Your phone." I tossed my head with a "duh" gesture.

"That's just gross." Mick laughed as he answered the call.

I could tell it was Teddy and it sounded like Mick would be going out on a call tonight after all. I stood wondering what he meant by "that's gross." I mean all I said was his butt dung—dung—Oh, I get it. I started giggling to myself as Mick hung up.

"What's up, babe?" I asked, feeling better already.

"I've got to go. An unhoused woman was found dead by the shelter," he said, leaning down to kiss me and rushing out the door.

Lia?

Chapter Four

After Mick left, I phoned Ava as I looped my tote handle over my shoulder.

"I just heard," she said in place of hello.

"How did you hear already?" I asked, getting in my car and heading toward her house.

"Police scanner. You picking me up or me you?"

"You have a police scanner? Since when?" I asked at a loss for words.

"It was my Valentine's Day gift from Delilah."

Odd gift, although I'm sure Ava asked for it. Thank God Delilah got my BFF. She's not all there—kind of like me.

"What are you doing? Are you still there? Hello? HELLO! JOLIE!"

"Good Lord, I'm here!"

"Why are you ignoring me?"

"I'm pulling in your drive now. Let's go."

Ava hung up and I assumed she was on her way out. I grabbed my two-ton tote to throw it in the back seat to make room for Ava as the passenger door swung open.

"That was rude to hang—" I started until I realized it was Delilah who got in and not Ava. "Oh, hey, where's Ava?"

"She's looking for her wallet. You know she's weird about leaving without it."

"Right," I said, rubbing my jean-covered thighs with my hands, something I did when I was nervous. I sensed Delilah had more to tell me. "What's up?"

"I don't want Ava doing this PI stuff anymore. It's getting too dangerous."

I sat in silence, feeling put in the middle of something. I didn't want to take sides or say the wrong thing. "I get you being nervous. You love her."

"I do. The longer I work with Nestle, the more of a dark feeling I get. He doesn't like you two and that in itself worries me."

Ava opened the back door. "You going with us?"

"You're welcome to," I said, hoping that would make Delilah feel better.

"Nah, I need to feed our babies. You get up here, sweets." Delilah held the car door open and pecked Ava on the cheek, then looked at me, pointing her finger. "I expect you to take care of her."

I nodded in agreement as I saw Ava roll her eyes.

"We'll be fine. The police will be there," Ava said, then slammed the car door.

I opted not to bring up Delilah's odd behavior and instead filled Ava in on Lia's visit to me earlier and how we need to find time to review everything and try to expose Nestle for the crook he is.

"Agreed," Ava gave me a one-word reply while reaching into her purse for some cheddar, peanut butter, and olive crackers.

"Delilah said you were looking for your wallet." I said as Ava offered me one of her snacks and I shook my head.

"Wasn't sure how long we'd be and wanted a snack." She sprayed bits of cracker out of her mouth as she spoke. Ava took a hard swallow as it dawned on her what I had just said about Lia. "Wait, you don't think—"

"Is it Lia? I don't know. But she tells me she's going back to pretending to be an unhoused person and almost immediately someone ends up dead." Tears welled up. I'd grown to like her as a friend. With everything we had been through together, she felt like a war buddy. And we both wanted Jackson Nestle to pay for his crimes.

I headed back the long newly paved road that led way back in the woods away from the interstate. Mayor Nalini insisted that he would only support this if the place was nowhere near the town or city. I had a feeling it was more the Tri-City mayor, John Cardinal, who wanted the unhoused residents hidden from sight. I'm sure he pressured Nalini to have the shelter be in Leavensport. He had been pushing people that struggled financially out of neighborhoods in Tri-City for the past year.

Heck, she and I had just worked together a few days ago—Lia used me as the go-between for her and Mayor Nalini to get the plans set for the Villy Crisis Center: A Helping Hand. We couldn't chance that Mayor Nalini knew who Lia was and would somehow tell Nestle, so she and I would meet and plan, and I would communicate with the mayor and relay the information to him as if it was my own idea. It was a complicated process, but worth it to keep Lia safe.

Lia came up with the name. She liked "villy," like "village," since it was for Tri-City and Leavensport people who struggled with keeping a roof over their heads. Mayor Nalini told me having something like "crisis center" in the title helped with grant money but Lia insisted on adding "a helping hand" so it didn't sound so forlorn in title alone. I pulled into the shelter parking behind Mick's truck, straightening out my arms on the steering wheel as I shook my blonde ringlets hard, forcing my brain to stop thinking of Lia in the past tense. I took a deep breath, preparing for the unknown.

"You ready?" Ava asked.

I nodded, feeling sick to my stomach. Ava and I hustled up the gravel drive and I saw my hubby and his co-workers had been hard at work securing the scene. There was yellow tape up, someone was photographing what I assumed was the covered body. That was probably Colleen taking the pictures. I noticed that she was careful to lift small parts of the cover so if any reporters were lurking around, they couldn't catch a good shot.

I saw a tall, muscular man in a white jumpsuit with booties on his feet and I knew that body regardless of what he was wearing. Mick was walking the perimeters with a flashlight, looking for evidence, careful of where he stepped. I was outside the tape and took my thumb and index finger and whistled low. Mick looked over his shoulder at me and I saw him shake his head as he ducked under the tape and moved carefully ten feet or so outside of the scene before walking in my direction.

"I should have known you two would follow me here," he sighed.

"We didn't follow you. I heard it on my—" Ava stopped herself.

"On your what?" Mick pulled his white hood down momentarily.

"Babe, I brought you a thermos with coffee and your pills. I didn't know how long you'd be." I zipped open my tote and pulled out the thermos and baggy with his nightly pills he took to help keep his MS at bay.

It seemed to distract him and remove some of the grump from his mood from finding us there. He took the thermos and poured a little coffee and sipped it. I handed him a bottle of water from the tote so he could take the pills.

"Good Lord, he's only fifteen minutes from home," Ava said, giving me a *thank you for saving me* look.

Mick wouldn't be thrilled to know she had a police scanner.

"I see the snoops are here."

I whirled around to see Jackson Nestle getting out of a white van.

"Who are you calling a snoop? Doesn't seem like a criminal should be flinging names around at law-abiding citizens." Ava took a few large steps toward him.

"Whoa!" Mick strode over and held her elbow. "I got this."

Mick walked over to Nestle's van as Teddy and Keith began moving from the crime scene toward us too.

Ava and I circled around the opposite side to get a peek inside the van.

"Geesh, and here I thought y'all didn't like me." Nestle grinned. "What happened here?"

"What are you doing here?" Teddy held a hand up making it clear Nestle shouldn't take another step.

"He has boxes in the back of his van," I yelled from the back. I cupped my hands around my face to get a better look in the windows.

"It's none of your business what I lug around, blondie," Nestle growled at me.

"Take it easy, pal." Mick took a step toward him.

Nestle put his hands up and retreated. "Sorry, but your little wifey has a tendency to butt into my business a little too often. A guy could get a complex."

"Believe me when I tell you, I would prefer to have nothing to do with you," I said flatly, crossing my arms over my chest.

"So don't." He glared.

"Wouldn't have to if you'd stay out of Leavensport," I countered.

"Free country. I can go where I please."

"Sure thing. You mind if we look at what's in the boxes?" Ava asked as she went to the back and began opening the van doors.

"Get your hands off this vehicle." Nestle strode from the passenger side to the back and clamped a hand around Ava's arm.

"Uh-uh, wrong thing to do!" A wave of rage hit me, and before I realized what was happening, I had charged him, smashing into him. He was much larger in stature than me, but I used my entire weight to slam into him, knocking him off balance. He dominoed into Ava, who shoved him back, then she lost her balance and fell on top of him.

Teddy, Keith, and Mick rushed over. Mick wrapped his arms around my middle, pulling me back as Keith took Ava's hands and pulled her up. Nestle lay there with a weird grin on his face.

"I'm pressing assault charges," Nestle said, reaching for Teddy to help him up. He didn't.

"So, you wouldn't want to tell us what's in those boxes, would you? I mean, I can have you stay here since it's a crime scene and get a warrant if necessary." Teddy stared down at him.

Nestle stood up, brushing dried leaves and grass off his clothing. "Hey, I don't mean to cause trouble. I'm here to drop off clothing and food. I've done it before. Go ahead and see for yourself."

Ava and I moved toward the van.

"The *police* can look. Not you two," Nestle yapped.

I stood back, arms crossed, glaring at him.

A few minutes later, the guys gave us a look and shook their heads.

"There's got to be something in there. Pull the van apart. He just happens to show up at the scene of a murder?" I said in disbelief.

"Whoa, what? Who was killed? Is that what's going on? Now I'll tell you if you want to search more you can get a warrant. No one told me someone was killed."

"What are you hiding?" Ava hollered.

"Nothing," Nestle said, "but I know you all would happily plant something on me. You need probable cause."

"You gave us permission," Mick said.

"That was before I knew someone was murdered here. No one bothered to tell me that." Nestle mimicked me, crossing his arms.

Teddy's mouth twitched and he looked from Mick to Keith. I could tell Nestle knew he had rights. Great.

"Hey, his right taillight is broken. You can cite him for that," I said to no one in particular.

"You'll have to bring your stuff back another time," Teddy said, ignoring my suggestion. "I don't want you going in there now. Also, I'd like you to stick around a little while. I'll have a few questions."

That gave me a tiny smidge of satisfaction. I tapped Mick on the shoulder and nodded my head toward my car as he and Ava followed me.

"You both need to work on controlling yourselves around him." Mick's voice was deep and husky, his dark eyes stormy looking from Ava to me.

"Sorry, I got a little hot under the collar," Ava said.

"Yeah, I'm sorry too. Can you tell us who the victim is?"

"Not right now," Mick said. "Why do you want to know so badly?"

"I don't want Nestle to know who it is if he wasn't involved. I mean, it depends on who it is," I stumbled on my words.

"Why?" Mick asked.

Mick knew Lia as Lia, the woman struggling with homelessness who started to turn her life around. I never told him she was Nestle's ex-wife that testified against him to get him put away in a white-collar prison in Canada for a small stretch of time which led to her having to be put in witness protection. This was one of those gray areas he and I had worked out in therapy. We decided that there would be things that we couldn't tell each other. Since Ava and I were licensed PI's now, we got to work a little more closely with the police, but not completely.

"Is it Natalia?" Ava asked.

"Who?" Mick asked.

"Lia," I said through gritted teeth, glaring at Ava.

Ava stood behind Mick, mouthing *sorry*.

"Wait, Lia's name is Natalia? Who's Natalia?"

"You have work to do. Is it Lia?" I asked again.

"Mick, we need you over here," Teddy yelled from inside the tape. "We found something."

"Gotta go." He leaned down to kiss me quickly and ran off, pulling his hood up.

I stood by the car as Ava opened the door to get in.

"You haven't told him about who Natalia is yet?" Ava asked.

"It's one of those gray areas," I said, looking at where the police were inside the tape, then seeing Nestle had settled in the driver's side of his van. I looked at the side door of the shelter for unhoused residents.

"What are you going to do?" Ava asked.

"There's a city cop stationed at the side door. I need to get in there to ask Devonte if he's seen Lia or not."

"You need me to create a distraction?" Ava

asked.

I nodded.

Ava started walking toward the officer as I moved up front to get in a hidden position that wasn't too far from the door.

"Ma'am, can I help you?" the officer asked.

Ava turned away from him and started moving toward the woods.

"Excuse me, ma'am. I need you to step this way." The officer reached for his belt.

Come on, Ava, don't spook him too much. My stomach lurched as I feared for my friend.

Ava bent over. "Help me, please," she yelled. "I'm pregnant. There's something not right." She groaned and sank to the ground, holding her belly.

The officer lifted his hand from his belt and ran to Ava, who had rolled over on her back and was flailing her limbs, reaching for the man and pulling at him. "Please help me!" she wailed.

Wow, she's good. I snuck to the door. Locked. *Dang it.* I knocked quietly, looking behind me. The officer was bent over Ava, who was looking at me. She wiggled, trying to get up, then fell back down, pulling the officer with her.

I jerked at the doorknob and knocked with a flat hand, mentally pleading, *please, anyone open the door.*

"Ma'am let me radio for help," the officer said.

I began to scoot back into the shadows when the door cracked open and I pushed my way through.

I shut the door quickly behind me, saying a quick prayer Ava got out of her predicament. I turned around to find one of the women from Tri-

City who periodically needed the shelter's services. "Jolie?" she said.

"Hey, have you seen Lia? Is she in here?"

The woman with the matted salt-and-pepper hair shook her head. "Not seen her. But Devonte's in back." She tipped back a bottle of something covered with a brown paper bag and gave me a toothless smile as she stumbled by me.

I couldn't help but notice the sour stench coming from her and my head jerked back as I was repulsed by the smell. Immediately, I felt my inner self scold my senses for my knee-jerk reaction. I'm sure she was new to this shelter and still learning the rules of what was and wasn't allowed here. Definitely, no alcohol. I shook it off and went to where she pointed, in search of Lia's friend.

"Jolie, girlfriend!" Devonte ran to me and squeezed me. "Girl," He took a deep, dramatic breath while waving his hand in front of his face, dark eyes wide. "It has been a day!"

"So, it's not Lia?" I asked.

"Huh? OH! WHOA! NOOOO." Devonte was horrified by the thought.

I felt my entire body unclench. "Is she in here? Nestle's outside."

"Haven't seen her." He peered around to make sure no one was listening and lowered his voice to a whisper. "She told me she told you what she's up to."

"She did, but I thought she'd be here."

"I haven't seen her for a day, but I know that's not her out there. That one hasn't been here long and she never said much to anyone."

"So, it's a woman, but you don't know who—just that it's not Lia." I scratched my head.

"Sorry darling, I have to go check on the bread I'm baking," Devonte said and rushed out of the room, leaving me standing there contemplating where Lia could be.

I went over to the side door, peeking out and seeing the guard back. *Okay, let me out!* I texted Ava, then waited. A few seconds later, the man grumbled under his breath and walk back over to my trouble-making accomplice. I inched over to the car and got in, then honked and yelled out the window as though I had been there the whole time. "AVA! Come on, Mick said we need to get out of here."

Ava had been slumped over again and quickly stood up, shaking the man's hand and rubbing his arm in thanks and speed-walking to the car.

"Thank you, sorry it took me so long!" I put the car in drive and started to pull out when Ava stopped me.

"Isn't that—"

We both squinted. "Luis—is that his name?"

"Nina's son, yeah, that's him. What on earth is he doing here?" Ava asked.

I put the car in park and we got out, calling his name. He was walking down the lane, looking like he was in a daze.

We ran to him and I touched his elbow. "Luis, it's Jolie and Ava. We met earlier at your mom's bakery. Are you okay? What's going on? Talk to us."

"I-I—IIIII..." He dragged the last 'I' out with index finger pointing back to where the dead body lay covered on the ground. His dark eyes were glazed over and blank. *Shock.*

"Luis," Ava barked, loudly snapping her fingers in front of his eyes. She held him by his shoulders and shook him hard. "Snap out of it. NOW!"

Luis shook his head sharply, then tilted his head as if seeing us for the first time. "You two, from—"

"Yes, it's Jolie and Ava. Now what's going on? Did you see what happened to that person?"

"I-I found her body. She, she was still trying to talk then she just—" He slipped back into a dazed silence again. Teddy ran up to them.

"There you are, son. I wondered where you ran off to. Now I need you to come back with me so I can ask you a few questions." Teddy reached for Luis.

Ava had her phone to her ear and took a large step in front of Luis, shaking a finger in the universal "no-no" gesture in Teddy's face. "Yeah, do you have her number? I need it. Her son is at the scene of a crime and the police are trying to question a minor. We need his mom here now."

Ava hung up the phone and went from having just been stern with Luis to protective by putting a reassuring arm around him. "You come with us and we'll wait until your mom gets here." Ava side-eyed Teddy as she moved Luis along with her, then glanced back at me saying, "Jolie, call the attorney, Mr. Mercurio, to make sure their rights are protected."

I obeyed in complete surprise by my bestie's ability to handle a situation and take care of a teen in need.

"Hey, Jolie, I have every right to ask a minor a general question. She didn't have to be like that." Teddy was not happy.

"You saw him, Teddy," I covered the mouthpiece of my cell with my hand as Mr.

Mercurio's number rang in my ear. "His complexion was palish green, he could barely speak. The kid was in shock. Ava was protecting him and you should be thankful. If you would have pushed that kid too hard, you could have found yourself—" The attorney picked up, interrupting my thought process with Teddy. He stomped off while I explained the situation to our town's attorney.

I slowly drove back up the long gravel drive thinking how much I hoped Luis would be okay after what he witnessed. He seemed like a good kid and he was so young to have to deal with seeing something like that. I needed to remember to talk to Nina about Tabitha so Luis could have access to a mental health professional to help him process the experience.

I grabbed the water bottle I had given Mick from on top of his truck and took a swig, surveying the situation. Luis waited in the back seat of my car as Ava stood guard outside the car to be sure no police tried to talk to him.

A car came speeding up the drive, sending puffs of dust and rocks flying everywhere. It turned sharply and the brakes squealed as the tires very nearly went through the yellow tape outlining the crime scene.

Nina jumped from the car, her face contorted into a mask of fear and the motherly instinct to protect her cub. She looked wildly at me.

I pointed to my car, not wanting to frighten the mother and helping her get to her child.

Luis jumped out of the car when he saw her and ran into the safety of her motherly arms.

Ava tilted a head toward the car, signaling me that it was time for us to leave.

Neither of us said much as we drove down the gravelly lane and headed into town. My mind was full of fading and hazy thoughts as I drove through town on autopilot.

"Jolie—" Ava started.

"Yeah," I said dully.

"I'm pregnant."

Chapter Five

I slammed on the brakes right in the middle of the road as my body froze in shock. Ava yelled, but the sound waves hit my ear in slow motion. "JOOOOOOLIEEEEEEEEE!"

Then, time snapped back like a rubber band. "What in the name of Hades are you doing?" Ava screeched, shoving on my arm. "Pull over! Do you need me to drive? You're going to get yourself, me, and my baby killed!"

Quickly, I looked in my rearview mirror. Luckily, it was the middle of the night by this time and no one was on the road. I realized I was sitting in front of the Leavensport Lions school district, and I pulled over into the large parking lot and took a few deep breaths.

"So, you weren't using a decoy when you told the deputy you were pregnant back here?" I asked thinking back to Ava on the ground with the cop leaning over her.

"Duh—I just told you I'm preggos!" Ava started then dived into more of an explanation. "Okay, so you know Delilah and I have been talking about kids and looking into ways we could have our own.

Well, we found something that worked, and voila!" Ava did jazz hands around her rotund middle area. The pickles and Almond Joy combo was making more sense now.

I took another puffy-cheeked deep breath and let out the air slowly. "I mean, that was last fall, then the marriage during the holiday season. I haven't heard either of you mention babies since then. Why didn't you tell me?"

"Of course you're going to make this all about you. I should have known," Ava huffed. I thought I noticed a tear in her eye as she turned her face away from me, looking out the window of the car.

Hormones already? I guess I didn't know how far along she was. "Ava, I'm sorry, let me start over. Congratulations! Seriously." I reached for her hand with one hand and reached across the console to rub her arm with the other hand.

"I'm sorry, I've just been so moody. My emotions are all over the place. I feel like I'm losing my mind. Seriously, Jolie, don't ever get pregnant. I'm not even that far along. We aren't telling anyone at this point. We want to wait until the twelve-week mark. Another month." Ava took a jagged breath in and let it out, blowing her nose hard.

"There's a goose on the loose," I squealed in the childish way we used to do as kids when one of us blew our nose.

We both cracked up laughing in the car and hugged. "I'm going to be the best auntie ever," I told her. "I'm going to make Lolly look like Humpty Dumpty after he fell off the wall."

"You bet you will!" Ava showed me the support I didn't deserve after my initial reaction. Then she turned her head and squinted. "Hey, isn't it kind of late for staff?"

I looked over to where Ava pointed. Three men or I guess it could be teens appeared to be coming out of the school building. I couldn't tell as dark as it was and we were parked in the back by the street. I put the car in drive and turned the lights on, slowly moving toward the small group.

"I wonder if it's kids doing a prank?" Ava said as we approached.

"Oh man, not you two!" an overgrown man-child said, slapping his pal on the shoulder haphazardly and jerking his thumb at us.

Mr. Cool-Hand Luke was none other than Caleb, the leader of Nestle's construction crew, and his side-kick, Asher. Unfortunately, I knew the pair all too well since they made it a point to stop in for breakfast at least three times a week. I swore it had to do with Nestle wanting someone to keep an eye on us.

"What on earth are the Belligerent Buddies doing out in the middle of the night at a high school?" Ava queried.

We'd made up the title for the guys since they seemed joined at the hip and were both as rude as two bulls in a china shop.

"So odd for you two to be nosing around in business that doesn't concern you," Caleb sneered. "Run along, little girls. Isn't it past your bedtime?" He made a dismissive gesture with his hand, as if we were children.

"Didn't I see you at Chocolate Capers recently?" I asked the third guy, the shorter man who I'd seen flirting with my friend Betsy about a week ago.

"He's Bobby Zane, the new principal here, what of it?" Asher crossed his arms.

"Do you need help?" Ava asked, leaning over me, peering up to Bobby, who seemed fidgety.

"No, these guys are here because..." he fumbled for words, looking from Asher to Caleb.

"We're going to do some work on the gymnasium. You know, construction stuff." Caleb pulled his loose-fitting jeans up around his waist, looking down at Bobby.

"Yeah, I've had a long day. They were supposed to meet me after school today, but something came up and I ran into them later and here we are. Hey, look at the time." Bobby rushed his words, looking quickly at his wrist, then putting his hand in his pocket.

He did the motion so quickly that I wasn't even sure he was wearing a watch.

"M-kay," I mumbled under my breath while side-eyeing Ava skeptically. I rolled up my window and drove off making a mental note to add Bobby Zane to our I-Spy Slides as suspicious.

The next morning felt like the movie *Groundhog Day* as I drove into Ava and Delilah's driveway and beeped twice to pick Ava up again, except this time for work. I'm sure she'd be just as exhausted as me since we got home so late last night.

True to the movie, Delilah came stomping toward me again, not looking any happier than she was last night when we both were in this same position.

"Hey, Jolie, we tried to call you to catch you but we had to leave a message," Delilah started as I looked at my phone, realizing I'd still had it on mute from when I went to sleep around two a.m., a few hours ago. "Ava's sick again this morning. I talked her into staying in bed. She said she'd come in a few hours if she's doing better."

"No worries. Has she had morning sickness for long?" I asked.

Delilah's mouth tightened and her lips went white. *Uh-oh.* "So, she told you. We said we weren't telling anyone *at all* until twelve weeks."

"I don't know that she would have told me except things got strange last night." I struggled to find the right words.

Delilah tapped her pretty Color Street Spring Daisies nails on the top of my side mirror. "That's why I told you I'm not comfortable with this PI business anymore. And it's not just because she's pregnant. I mean, it's that too, but she's going to be a mom—we're going to be moms. So, someone else who can't fight for themselves is going to be our responsibility."

"Say no more. I get it. I really do. I haven't had a ton of time to digest anything yet, but I do hear you. I will take the time to think about it and I'll take care of it. I promise. I mean, I can't have my little niece or nephew in danger now, can I?" I looked up, smiling at her with my face, but internally I was nervous as I knew I'd still have to solve the case. I'd never known Ava to allow anyone, including me, to tell her what she could or couldn't do. But under the piercing green-blue eyes of Delilah, I felt obliged to say the right things. "Also, if she needs to stay home today, it's no trouble. I can call in the Tucker Calvary if I get in over my head at the restaurant."

I arrived at Cast Iron Creations and was doing

the normal morning routine of lights, chairs, coffee brewing, prepping for breakfast while simultaneously rethinking the events of the last few days.

Another violent murder in our town. Too much had been going on over the holidays with the double wedding, selling my house, finding a house, moving in with Mick while Delilah moved in with Ava, not to mention helping Lia set up the shelter. We really needed to find time to look over our I Spy Slides and the connections to the mafia and what we recently found out about what went on in Leavensport in the late nineties.

I counted out twelve to-go boxes and began the breakfasts for the regulars, realizing I'd forgotten the greatest surprise for me was my best friend was pregnant. She had told me, but I hadn't processed it completely. Plus, I needed to think about what Delilah said. Ava was out there with that cop last night risking her and the baby's health trying to help me get inside the shelter.

A loud knock at the door up front startled me as I was boxing the last of the breakfasts. Quickly, I peered down at my watch. It wasn't time to open yet. I picked up the warmer bag and put the boxes in it and wiped my hands on my apron, moving through the double swinging doors of the kitchen to the dining area. I saw Tom Costello with hands clasped, peering in the glass door.

I waved at him as I made a beeline to the cuddly cubicle, as I liked to call it, where we had a bench, big fluffy pillows and books on a bookshelf. The bench allowed guests to sit, read, and sip tea while enjoying the art gallery lane, which was always beautifully decorated by Delilah and her art students. I pushed two books into the shelf and straightened the pillows and then jogged to the door.

"Sorry, I know you're not open yet," Tom said, taking his tweed brown walrus hat off as he stepped inside.

"Coffee's brewing, want a cup?"

"That would be wonderful, thanks."

I poured a cup for Tom and grinned awkwardly. "What's up?"

"Um, I can't seem to get your grandma to give me the time of day. I hate to get you involved but I know she favors you. I don't suppose you'd be willing to talk to her for me?" Tom sipped his coffee with one hand while restlessly rubbing the back of his neck with the other.

I looked down at my hands, picked up a stool to sit, then changed my mind and pushed the stool to the side. "Yeah, I'm sorry. I'm not comfortable getting in the middle."

Tom looked crestfallen.

"Listen, you know Grandma. She's stubborn. Way more obstinate than most people. So, she needs more time than most people do."

Tom shifted on the stool. "That's true. It's just she yelled at me during the holidays to explain but never gave me the chance. Now, she's refused to look at me since then. She won't take my calls, emails, texts, visits."

"She doesn't understand. She thought you were one person and found out you were someone else." I bit my lip feeling an eency-weency bit bad for being so blunt with him.

"I'm not proud of some of the things I've done in my past, but I've paid for all that. I'm not the same man I was then."

"Who were you?" I demanded. "That's part of the problem, Mr. Costello. We were told you were the reason Karl was put in prison all those years for something he didn't do. It seemed like you were having illegal raves or something in the tunnels below your store. And you aren't denying anything or explaining anything!" I realized I was badgering him.

Tom exhaled a huge breath. "I'm happy to sit down with you, your grandma, and the entire Tucker clan and explain things the best I can. Just ask her . . . please?"

I looked up, seeing my regulars form a line at the door, then looked at my watch, realizing I was a few minutes late opening again. "I have to open up now. I'll talk to her and try to get her to talk to you." I jogged to the door to unlock it but before turning the lock I looked back at Tom and said, "But no promises."

I had rushed to get the regulars rang up and out the door to their jobs on time and started taking orders and throwing eggs, bacon, sausage, flapjacks, and the like together in the skillets in the back. I'd thought Ava was going to run the front of the store and I got so lost in thought I hadn't contacted my family or Magda to see if she could come in early.

I looked up, panicky, as the bell to the front door dinged yet again. I let out a breath as I saw Mrs. Seevers walk in with Caleb and Asher. I wasn't thrilled to see the Belligerent Buddies, and I did briefly wonder what on earth Mrs. Seevers would have to talk about with them, but she loved to chit-chat and probably would with nearly anyone. I was happy to see her, though.

"Mrs. Seevers!" I hollered from the kitchen as

she waved sweetly to the guys and rushed back to me.

"What's going on, sweetie?"

"Ava is under the weather and I don't have help. Could you please—"

"Say no more, dear." Mrs. Seevers grabbed an apron, ordering pad, and pen. She got two more pots of coffee going, then took the other pots of decaf and regular around to fill up cups, telling others she'd be right with them to take their order.

What a lifesaver. Ava and I had had her working part-time for us in the past, so she knew the drill.

There was finally a lull and I gave Mrs. Seevers a hug. "Thank you so much! I was drowning there for a minute."

"Oh, you would have been fine. I'm happy to help! So, did you hear about last night?"

"Um yeah, it's horrible."

"I heard that they recently got cameras up for security reasons but had them set in weird spots," Bea said. "Supposedly, they have two suspects on camera. Did Mick say who they are?"

I tried to suppress a smile. That's why she was here—she wanted the scoop. "I got in late last night and he got in even later than me. I was asleep when he got in and the same thing happened in the morning. When I left, he was asleep. I'm afraid I don't know."

"Hello, we need more coffee here!" Asher yelled across the restaurant from their corner table.

Mrs. Seevers started to jump up from the stool.

"Nope," I said. "I got it."

I plastered on a fake smile and forced my

shoulders back, attempting to prevent my eyebrows from twitching with annoyance. I went over and quickly refilled the cups at the guys' table and tore off the check and laid it near Asher, not asking if they'd like anything else then said, "I didn't think I'd have the pleasure of seeing you two again so soon!"

"Don't expect a tip with how slow the service was here," Caleb mumbled ignoring my remark but commenting loud enough for me to hear.

I kept my back turned to him, moving down the row of tables and filling up some other empty cups. I saw Mr. Seevers had walked in and sat next to his wife, who reached over to pour him a cup of coffee.

"Hey, Mr. Seevers," I said, sitting the pot down to take his order.

"Did those guys know anything about who was on the tape?" Mrs. Seevers asked.

"Didn't ask them," I said, grinning at Earl Seevers.

"Bea, mind your own business," he shushed her.

I ran back to pull a savory ham, cheese, onion, and bell pepper quiche out of the oven as the two bickered at the counter.

"Where have you been, anyways?" Bea asked her husband as I brought a couple pieces of quiche out to them. She turned to me. "Oh Jolie, this looks delightful!"

"Thanks, it's on the house. Your wife saved my skin this morning."

"She's a keeper." He rubbed his wife's knee. "To answer your question, I found out an old friend is back in town."

"Who?" Mrs. Seevers and I said in unison. As much of a busybody as I thought she was, I had to accept I was just as bad.

"Harvey Tobias."

Mrs. Seevers didn't seem thrilled, but I wasn't sure if she was upset with her husband being late or at Mr. Tobias turning up in town.

I was getting ready to ask her if she was okay when Asher yelled out, "Hey, does anyone work here? We'd like to-go cups for our coffee, please!"

I tipped my head from side to side to loosen my neck as Magda came in for her shift.

"I got it, Jolie," Magda said, running back to get her gear as Ava slowly trudged in behind her.

"Thanks," I said, noticing Magda had changed the spiky blue tips of her hair to a neon green.

"You didn't have to—" I started but Ava rushed to the bathroom.

"Is she okay?" Mrs. Seevers asked.

"I think she has that stomach flu that's been going around," I stalled, watching Ava come out and move through the kitchen to the office. I followed her.

"I told Delilah you didn't need to come in today. Go home and rest," I said.

Ava shook her head, then stopped and put her hand on her stomach with an introspective look and a pause. "I'm okay. Supposedly, this is all normal for the first trimester. I can't just stay in bed for nine months."

I found myself trotting after Ava again as she walked back to the counter to make herself a cup of decaf tea.

I picked out a peppermint teabag and handed it

to her. "Supposed to settle your stomach."

"Who's the hulked-out supermodel talking to your hubby outside?" Ava asked, dunking the teabag in hot, steamy water.

I did a rubberneck. I saw Mick outside across the street. Sure enough, he was standing near a woman, but her back was to me so I couldn't see who it was.

"I'll go see who it is," Bea said, jumping from her stool, pushing through the door, and taking big strides toward Mick and the supermodel.

I looked panic-stricken at Ava, who just shrugged her shoulders nonchalantly. I went out, following Mrs. Seevers. On our way out, we passed my mom, aunt, and Grandma Opal, who were going *into* the restaurant. "Excuse me," I said, squeezing past them, looking both ways, and crossing the street, forgetting I was still wearing my You've Got to Be Kitten Me apron with a fluffy pink kitten on it playing with black fuzzy yarn.

I suddenly sensed I had additional followers so I glanced over my shoulder. Apparently my mom, aunt, and grandma had done an about-face and followed me back out of the restaurant like a bunch of baby ducks trailing after their mama. Ava had come too, even waddling a little as she brought up the rear, just to complete the image. Mick's face was beet red as he looked at the small crowd gathering. Now I felt foolish as I stood at a loss for words.

The woman had legs that didn't stop. She wore a tight black miniskirt with spike-heeled princess sandals. Her hair was thick, dark, and naturally curly. She had a face out of *Gone with the Wind*, with pouty lips, delicate hands, and curves in all the right places. Her neon green tank top showed off her well-defined biceps. She hadn't even spoken and I hated her. Her lithe figure, even the muscles in her shoulders and back complimented her designer outfit perfectly.

"What's up?" Mick's ears turned red.

I'm sure no one else noticed, but when my hubby got embarrassed, the tips of his ears always turned red. Looks like the Tucker women continued to make men shake in their boots.

"Oh—uh—well, Mrs. Seevers was coming over to ask you a question, then I realized I knew the answer. So, I came after her. And them..." I jerked my thumb behind me, "...they came in to see me and they...also followed." I started the sentence standing tall and by the end of the last phrase my shoulders were sagging in defeat.

"Nice apron," the princess said, grinning at me. "What's in your hair?"

Of course, she had a heavy, sexy Italian accent too.

"My?" I reached for my head feeling a huge glop of something sticky.

"Oh, Jolie, you got raw egg in your hair again," Aunt Fern said, reaching in her pocketbook for a pick and ripping the prongs through my matted hair, yanking my head sideways.

"OW!" I yelled, jerking away as a huge chunk of hair came out into her pick.

The woman giggled under her breath.

"Jolie, this is Imelda. She's a friend from childhood." Mick tried to ignore the comic scene. "And this is my wife, Jolie."

Mick had moved next to me, putting his strong arm around my waist and patting at my gloppy hair mess as he grinned down at me.

I reached a hand out to Imelda. Wow, she smelled amazing. Was it possible that she smelled even better than she looked? "It's so nice to meet you. Sorry for this," I took both my hands to frame my entire self, head to toe.

I noticed Imelda had a huge black leather headband with a large red flower done in leather wrapped around her long locks. It was very unique, chic. Better than egg.

"Oh, you are Jolie. Okay, it all makes sense now." She smiled.

"What makes sense?" I felt my voice waver into a singsong as I asked the question. My blue eyes darted back and forth and my mouth grew straight-lipped.

"We need to get back to help Magda." Ava pulled on my arm as Mick reached down for a quick kiss.

My fan club followed as Mick yelled out, "Mrs. Seevers, what were you going to ask me?"

I stopped and we all turned around.

"It can wait." She turned to me and shrugged as we all scooted into the restaurant.

"I don't like her," my grandma snarled once we got inside.

"Who, Mama Opal?" Ava asked.

"Matilda," Grandma said.

"Who? I-MEL-DA?" I pronounced each syllable slowly.

"Whoever, she's up to no good with Mick. You best keep an eye on that one!"

Bea waved down the women in my family and brought them to a table, beckoning Earl to join them.

I went back to the kitchen to start on some orders while Magda continued with the few tables up front.

"Since we both are off at the same time today, I thought I'd come over to your place so we can finally sit and revisit our slides," Ava said, sitting at the office desk with the door propped open so we could talk.

"You know," I took a deep breath. "I've got to get these orders up then get this gunk out of my hair. But I think it's best if we just let the police handle this one." I turned my back to her when I saw her face cloud over.

I got home from work later that afternoon and immediately fed the kitties, scratched some furry little heads, and gave them clean water. After that, I went around scooping out litter boxes and sweeping up loose litter. Then saw the note from Mick.

Sorry we missed each other last night and this morning.

Also, sorry for the weirdness this afternoon. I got

some lunch and won't be home until around nine tonight.

I winced, wishing we could take time to talk but trusting we would get to it later. Then, I looked around at the mess that still needed to be sorted. So much more unpacking to do. I spent a couple of hours unpacking, cleaning, organizing the last few unpacked boxes. It was soothing—exactly what I needed. I always felt better when things had order and were organized.

It was only six in the evening. I made a grilled

cheese and grabbed some Doritos and a Coke Zero and went to the couch, opened my laptop, and clicked on the I Spy Slides document. I reached for my tote and pulled out my journal to take some notes.

"Alexa, play Ella Fitzgerald."

"Play-ing Ella Fitz-gerald," Alexa replied.

The first thing I noted was that Lia was back undercover but no one seemed to know where she was located. This was day two of her being missing, if she was.

Next, I opened the document called "Goodfellas," which was a flowchart of all the connections Ava and I had found to the mafia. So far, we'd figured Jackson Nestle was connected to the Canadian group and had connections to Mick's family—the Sicilian mafia. For a quick minute, we feared Ava's family was mixed up in the Dominican Republic mafia but found out it was other families that the Martinezes had worked with in the past.

That's three—I used my stylus pen and circled the Irish name of Liam on the slide, not sure what to make of that, but then I added a new section and labeled it "Leavensport mafia" with a huge question mark. I shivered. I still couldn't believe someone in our village was connected to this. So far, Tom Costello seemed to be the most likely. That made me wonder why I'd promised to try and get grandma to listen to him. Although, he did offer to speak to all of us. Maybe he could shed some light on all this.

I heard a key rattling in the door and sat up, wondering why Mick was home early. Instead, Ava came barreling through the door with a family-sized bag of marshmallows in one hand and a large pickle jar under her other arm. Her purse was hanging down around her wrist and she had a brown bag hanging from her teeth.

"What on earth?" I pushed the stuff off my lap and jumped up to help her. I pulled the bag from her teeth and took the marshmallows, allowing her to reposition her purse.

"Whew, thanks." Ava swung the purse on the chair and sat the pickle jar on the coffee table.

"How did you get a key to our house?" I stood, hands on hips, as Ava reached for the marshmallows.

"Why shouldn't I have one?" Ava's nostrils were flaring. "You have a key to my house and I used to have one to yours. What's the big deal?"

I scratched my head. "Again, *why* do you have a key to our house and *how* did you get it?"

"I mean, I may have told Marty that you gave me one and I lost it." She popped a pillowy white marshmallow in her mouth and chased it with a bread-and-butter pickle.

I felt bile rise to my throat. I'm sure that was from the disgusting food combo I was forced to watch and not the stomach flu. Marty was a kind older member of our community who'd known us since birth. Of course, he would never question Ava. He knew our families were close and Ava and I even closer in friendship.

"So, you lied to the man." I stood, arms crossed, tapping my foot. "Let's say Mick was home and we had decided to have some romantic time over there on the table and you just barged in."

"Um, first off, it's not Saturday night, so I know you wouldn't be doing the nasty with your man. Second, puleaassse, Jolie, as if you'd ever do it anywhere but a bed." Ava rolled her eyes, stuffing more buttery goopy juice in her mouth.

"Okay, that is just rude. You do not know our sex schedule—"

"I do. You told me before," Ava said in triumph.

"Just because I may have said something doesn't make it true!" I threw my hands up.

"And you're calling me a liar?"

I pressed my tongue to the roof of my mouth, hands in pockets, shoulders hunched, eyes looking at the ceiling.

"I came here to tell you Bradley told me who is on the video. The one you told me Bea was talking about earlier but—hey, you have your notes out and mafia slides up. You told me we were letting the police handle it!"

Wow, I really was a horrible liar. "You know—Mick left a note he'll be home late. So, I thought I'd take a quick look until he gets home."

"Oh really, so, this list of questions here: *Where's Lia? Who is the dead woman? What does Nestle have to do with it? Principal with construction guys?* That isn't you putting together a list before you start investigating? Because I'm the one who started the PI business. Not you."

Oh boy, Ava looked hurt. Which, to me, was worse than mad.

I tilted my head and attempted to run my fingers through the curls but there was still a bit of egg from earlier. "I didn't want to tell you this—" I started.

Ava's large dark eyes looked up at me in pain. She normally wasn't this emotional.

"Delilah is worried about you and the baby. She

talked to me about it and I agree with her. I think I can handle this one on my own but it just occurred to me that you could help with things like this—where it's safer." I bit the inside of my cheek and breathed after spitting all that out quickly.

"I knew it!" Ava yelped. "How could you or she question that I'd endanger this little one? That is absolutely ridiculous. There are women who are pregnant all over the world with dangerous jobs and they don't quit."

"True, but it's not like you're a trained cop, Ava. We stumbled into this. You did an online program and Tabitha helped pushed things through. We aren't the most experienced PI's around."

Ava pulled out her phone and dialed, standing to pace the floor as it rang. "Baby, can you come to Jolie's so we can all talk?"

I shook my head. Oh man, I should have kept lying.

"Huh? Okay, we'll see you then."

There was a knock at the door as Ava hung up. "Was she already here?"

"No, she's in the middle of something and will be here within the hour."

I opened the door to see Tabitha staring at me with blank eyes.

"Hey, come on in," I said, peering at Ava, whose one eyebrow was arched.

"You okay?" Ava asked.

"The dead woman—it was my cousin, Janelle."

Chapter Six

I started the tea kettle and got three cups ready, then took a box of tissues over to the sitting area. Ava and I sat waiting until Tabitha felt ready to share with us. She was shaken and we weren't used to seeing her this way.

"Janelle was six years younger than me. She'd always looked up to me and that's why she worked to get into the FBI. When I moved here, she moved into my old position, doing undercover work on mafia connections."

"Oh wow, I'm so sorry." I started to reach for her but she pulled away, shaking off the emotion.

"I'm on the edge. I know you two can get around some legalities that I can't," she muttered, with a look on her face I had never seen before. "They crossed the wrong person. I'll stop at nothing to get these scumbags. This is ten years I've been involved with this and now someone strangled my cousin. Janelle was trained. Whoever did this had to be stronger and taller than her to bring her to her knees and I found out the rope burns shifted up so they stood over her." I noticed her hands were knotted in fists as if she were visualizing her cousin's murder and she was shaking in a terrifying way.

"So, you've been doing undercover work while in Leavensport?" I verbalized my shock. I felt confused and embarrassed, remembering all the times I had dumped my darkest secrets out to an undercover cop.

Tabitha stared straight at me, giving me back that stern, straight-lipped gaze and said, "I *am* a therapist. I could be in big trouble if I wasn't. But yes, I am here, as I said, as a part-time therapist, helping Teddy out as he needs it consulting on some cases—what you didn't know is that consultation ties into all the crime that has been taking place here in town."

Ava and I glowered.

"You helped us become PI's. You allowed Jolie to talk to you about her most private thoughts and feelings. You talk to Mick about his as well. You may know some of the things you know from your sessions with Jolie. That seems like a conflict of interest," Ava said. She was such a good investigator. That hadn't even occurred to me.

"Wait, does Mick know and has he known this entire time that you are undercover?" I felt sick to my stomach again. This all was too much to process. I mean, I felt for Tabitha. She just lost a family member in a very violent way, but I also felt betrayed and confused first by her and now I was left wondering how much Mick knew this entire time.

Tabitha took a deep breath, sat up straight, and licked her top lip. "Jolie, I'm sorry. This is all coming out wrong because I'm so emotional right now. I promise you I did not use you in any way. If you remember, there were times you tried to share things with me *in the office during a session* and I changed the subject. But there were times we ran into each other in town, and yes, I did get any information I could get out of you then."

Whoa. I took a breath. I glanced at Ava, who looked ticked.

"So, basically you helped us become PI's to help you along in your investigation? AND NOW, you are asking us to bend the law for you too? And yeah, DID Mick know all this?" Ava stood and started pacing again.

Tabitha looked helpless.

"Okay, I'm sorry. I'm doing all the things I tell my patients not to do—reacting with emotion and no logic. Of course, I should have never said you two could skirt around legalities. I'm sorry. I don't know what's come over me. You know what, there is going to need to be a time when you, Mick, Ava, Delilah, and I need to sit and discuss this whole thing, but it's not tonight." Tabitha's voice quivered.

I gave Ava a look that said *let it drop for now* and got the tea ready to serve.

"I'm sorry, this is cold now. I can heat it up in the microwave." I collected our mugs.

"Don't worry about it," Tabitha said and blew her nose. "We will all talk through this. Please don't be mad at Mick, though. I wish—I wish—oh, I don't know, I wish everything were different."

Then something I never thought I'd see happen happened. Tabitha crumpled into a pillow on my couch and began sobbing uncontrollably. That is something I'd done once with her and also got at least a little teary-eyed almost every single session, but she was always the rock. I froze. I looked to Ava. She was motionless, with only her large brown irises moving between me and Tabitha.

Ava and I both caved and went to comfort her. "Seriously, you have enough to worry about. Do not worry about me and Mick. Even if he knew, we'll work through it. I'm sure it's all complicated. Right now, what do you want to do? Why are you telling us everything now?"

Tabitha sat up, apologized awkwardly, then got herself together. "I guess, wow, this feels weird to say, but I never saw any of this coming—obviously, but with Janelle—I just want to—"

"To get to the bottom of what's going on in Leavensport and who's behind murdering your cousin," Ava finished her statement for her.

Tabitha nodded, wiping her nose with a Kleenex.

"Are you up for discussing a few things now?" I asked.

"That's why I'm here."

"But are you willing to share with us now?" Ava asked.

"I can help you with some things," Tabitha said.

Ava's cheeks turned maroon.

"Again, we'll talk more about what you can and can't share later when we are all together." I gave Ava a repetitive glance from earlier.

"Okay, what I can share right now is that those tunnels connected to Tri-City are key in the history of all of this. Dating all the way back to the 1920's."

"Why the 1920's? Do you know?" I asked.

"I do know. Or at least, I think I know. I'm not sure if I can tell you that, though. I can tell you that you can look at what was going on in the twenties and take a pretty good, educated guess, though."

"Okay, I love a good mystery," Ava said, typing that into the notes of one of our slides.

There was a knock at the door and I looked quizzically at Ava.

"It's Delilah." Ava went to the door.

"WAIT!" Tabitha said urgently. "I know I've already asked for so much from you two. Can you not share any of this with Delilah or Mick until we all sit down together to talk?"

There was a beat of silence before a louder knock on the door.

Ava and I contemplated with facial expressions that only people that were raised together could figure out. Then we both nodded, although our expressions conveyed our skepticism. We had agreed—for now.

As Delilah came in, Tabitha gathered her things and hugged us both. "Thank you both for being here. I promise we'll talk soon. Delilah, I'm sorry I can't stay."

"Sorry, I didn't know she was here," Delilah said after I shut the door behind Tabitha.

"It's okay, it's been a long day," Ava said, rubbing her belly wearily.

"You doing okay?" Delilah asked.

"I guess. Why did you tell Jolie you didn't want me involved in investigations? I mean, why wouldn't you share that with me?"

I squirmed in my seat taking a huge gulp of my cool tea.

"I—I don't know. I guess I—"

"You knew I wouldn't be happy with you dictating what I should and shouldn't do. You knew

Jolie was the next best thing to control me. Is that it?" Ava was back to standing and pacing again.

"I don't think that's what she meant. I mean, I get why—" I started.

"No, Jolie, she's right. I didn't want her in danger and I knew she wouldn't listen," Delilah said to me, then turned toward Ava. "But you are carrying our child. That gives me a right to worry about both of you. Things are different now."

"They really are," I agreed.

"Seriously, you both are going to gang up on me now?"

"I won't be able to not worry about you even if all you do is work at the restaurant," Delilah said.

"I know. I am who I am. I want this baby. I want us to have a family. I want to keep both my jobs. I realize the PI work does put me in more danger. I plan to be careful." Ava stood, hands on hips.

"Okay, is there anything that would make you feel better? A compromise of some sort?" I asked. I was getting really good at this therapy stuff.

Delilah shrugged her shoulders as her long light brown waves cascaded around her perfect, rosy, porcelain cheeks. "I don't want to be a PI, but I feel involved with Nestle buying into my business and being married to a PI who runs two businesses with her best friend who is married to the town's detective, so—"

"So, you want in on the investigations?" Ava asked.

"I think at least while you're pregnant. After that, I would need to wait and see. Again, this is not something I'm interested in—the last time I got involved, I ended up with a Canadian mobster involved in my family's businesses."

Ava's shoulders slumped, as did mine as we both knew she was referring to when she helped Ava's family get out of a dangerous debt. Delilah became someone she wasn't to help the woman she loved. Which, thinking back to Delilah's use of that gun, made me shudder all over. It would be terrifying to have her involved. When she went into protective mode, she was ferocious.

"First things first," I said. "I'm sharing our I Spy Slides with you." I reached for the computer.

"I'm sorry, the what?" Delilah asked.

Ava filled her wife in on the name we had for tracking each investigation separately and the document we had for all the connections to the mafia ties to Leavensport.

Delilah grinned but also seemed impressed at the same time.

"Well, let's add that Nestle seemed stalled for a while. I hadn't seen or heard from him in months. The last few weeks, he's showing up again."

"Why don't you note when you remember him backing off and when he started showing up," I said, handing the laptop to her. "Also, you and Ava can go over everything we've figured out so far at home. I need to look over it all again too."

"Something else I overheard at the craft store was that Teddy's dad, Harvey, is back in town," Delilah said. "There's been all kinds of rumors that have floated around about him. Bea Seevers was the one talking to one of her cronies, telling her that Harvey was forced to retire because of some unscrupulous activities while acting as chief and the mayor at that time wanted to cover it all up."

"Who was the mayor then?" I asked. I thought

back to when I was a kid and Ava and I used to go over to the Tobiases' house to play balloon stomp and have sack races. Harvey always refereed with a funny polka-dotted shirt, clown wig and shoes, and a loud whistle. He had us all in stitches. It was difficult for me to picture him in a sinister light.

"Not sure, but that's something we can easily find out," Delilah said.

Ava and Delilah headed out as my brain spun in twenty directions. I started unpacking more boxes while talking to Bobbi Jo, who seemed to be watching over me, making sure I didn't mess anything up. "What's wrong with you? Are you mama's boss or something?" I scratched her little calico head as her bobtail jiggled.

About an hour later, Mick came in looking exhausted. I didn't like that I had mixed feelings about him right now and I couldn't talk to him about it yet. I smiled as naturally as I could.

"Sorry I'm late. It's this case," he said, dropping his keys and wrapping his arms around me. "How was your day?"

I kept my head buried in his shoulder. "Pretty uneventful day." I hated lying to him.

Chapter Seven

Usually, mornings are a crazy rush. I'm normally lugging my tote around my shoulder, eating a granola bar with no hands and scratching kitty heads with both hands as I sprint out the door. Part of the time I'm half-dressed, buttoning and zipping things as I steer with my knees, all the while picking my hair out with my "free" hand that probably *should* be on the steering wheel.

But today when I opened my eyes from a deep sleep, for the first time in a long time, I saw a very clear and beautiful sky. Mick had left for work. The past few days seemed to have had dark clouds over them. I picked up my journal, thinking I could write in it to relax before running my errands on this lackadaisical morning. I'd swapped shifts with Carlos today and was closing tonight. He volunteered to work an extra three hours for overtime, and I took him up on it. I opened my journal, deciding to try my first freewriting assignment Ava had given me. She liked to study the newest procedures in the private investigative world. She told me when I was stuck in a case a strategic way to work through problems was to do freewrite journaling. She'd tried it and it helped her. So, I read about the process and figured it couldn't hurt. I had a history of journaling anyways.

I'm still feeling that Carlos isn't telling me and Ava everything. He's always trusted us in the past. It's not like him to keep something from us. He's only feeding us bits and pieces. Why? Who cares? He knows we'd do anything for him. So, it's something big. Something is scaring him. Someone is scaring him. Is it the person who is the mastermind in Leavensport? Or are they using a puppet to mask their identity from Carlos? Wait, is that what they have been doing this entire time? Denise never knew who was blackmailing her either.

What did Tabitha say last night? Something about being able to look up the answer—answer for what? Too many things were happening and my brain was overworked.

Oh right, the tunnels. They were first noticed in the 1920's and while she couldn't tell us the reasoning, she said anyone could look it up.

Okay . . .

I ran out to get my laptop, which was still sitting on the coffee table from last night and ran back to the bedroom, jumped under the sheets and arranged my pillow, setting up the laptop, then flipped it on—black screen.

"Man!" I declared to no human. "Battery's dead." I slapped my leg, looking my Lenny Lee right in his little black and white Oreo face as he blinked his eyes at me in understanding.

I threw the sheet off in frustration, dragged my legs over the side of the bed, and reached for the charging cord, leaning the front side of my body off the mattress, ever so careful to not actually touch the floor—because any sane person knows you are still considered IN BED as long as NO PART OF YOUR BODY touches the floor and anything you do in that time means it's not an actual chore—and I plugged the computer in.

Before looking up the history of the twenties, I wrote a quick thought.

Note to self: Jolie, when you complain that two businesses is too much, remember the absolute nonsense that pops into your brain when you have nothing to focus on.

That felt better, tick that little tidbit off my list. I looked up some history and the biggest topics I found tied into the constitution being amended twice, women's right to vote, and some guy named Ponzi came up with a scheme.

Hmmm. I spent a bit of time reading about the Ponzi scheme, thinking it had to be something nefarious to tie into the use of the tunnels and the mafia from somewhere. Okay, this stuff was a scheme but wasn't mob-level trouble. Plus, nothing to hide or smuggle in tunnels.

I scrolled the screen, skimming about women's right to vote, feeling a glint of pride as a registered voter. *Oh. Okay. Here's something*, I thought to myself, reaching for my journal and shifting from freewriting to note-taking by assigning a title to each. Hopefully, Ava never saw this or she'd never let me live down my obsession with all things list-and-organization-related.

The amendment to the Constitution—I hadn't seen what was amended. I looked at the word and wrote it in my journal.

Prohibition . . . tunnels. Okay, that answers for the 1920's but what about 1997?

I hesitated for a moment then glanced at the clock. Wow, normally time flew but only twenty minutes had passed by and I felt a rush of warmth flow through me, realizing I could continue to lounge in my book boxers and Kool Kat tee. Back to freewriting now.

1997. What was happening then that tunnels could have been used for? They were calling it construction then but it was something more.

Carlos had mentioned last December when we were talking about uses of the tunnels that Princess Diana died in the horrific car crash in 1997. Carlos.

Carlos.

Carlos.

Carlos.

Carlos, Oh, right! Carlos, that's where I started with all this. Carlos isn't telling us everything because he's afraid of someone or something. It's got to be something big. Like family. He said something a while back when he was afraid. What did he tell me? Something I didn't understand, about how his family needed to get here. He had to find a way to get his family here. Someone's blackmailing him—the same someone's who blackmailed Keith's sister, Denise. Except we never found out who it was. Denise never knew their identity. But Carlos knows. And I'll bet this house and home that whoever runs this three-ring mafia scam in Leavensport is behind it and they are pulling some strings. Maybe they offered to smuggle Carlos' family into the states in exchange for him doing something for them? I mean, Mary told me that—that she thought something was going on with his family.

The other thing I struggled to understand was Tom Costello's role in it all. Now, Harvey, Teddy's dad, is back in town and there are different rumors flying around. Delilah said she had heard Harvey had taken early retirement because the mayor at the time wanted to cover some things up. There were some corrupt activities going on with the mayor while Harvey was acting chief. I wonder who she heard that from???

I looked above to my list for *NOTES* and added a bullet point to find out who was the mayor at that time—of both Leavensport and Tri-City.

Later that morning, I headed over to my friend Betsy's shop, Chocolate Capers to pick up three raspberry chocolate tortes that Betsy made for cross-selling with us this week. Most merchants in our town were on a schedule that I kept track of, where we exchanged our products and sold them in our shops to cross-sell. We started this back when we first heard most of the fields leading up the highway toward Tri-City were going to be sold off for businesses. The hope was that as more people opened businesses within our village limits, they would be involved in town meetings and in cross-selling. It would help to keep the locals' businesses alive and not eaten up by new businesses. Knowing I could sleep in this morning, I had stayed up late last night making three Gooey Texas Chocolate Sheet Cake Skillets for Betsy to sell.

I had the cakes in a warmer bag and was juggling my tote and the door. Betsy was glued to the window behind the counter.

"What are you looking at?" I asked, nearly tumbling over as the door swung hard from the wind and knocked my behind, propelling me forward. Somehow, the gods must have been watching, because I caught my footing and managed to not fall and destroy the cakes. This was usually not the case.

"Oh, geesh, I'm sorry. So sorry." Betsy ran around the counter to take the bag from me. "I saw Teddy across the street and was going to holler and ask him to come over. I wanted to ask him how his dad is doing and how their relationship is since he's back in town."

Betsy arranged a few glass cake stands with decorative blown glass flowers around the edges that were so lustrous and glossy they resembled chocolate themselves. She pulled the chocolate sheet cakes out and her green eyes widened. "Jolie, these look fabulous!"

"Thanks, I tried out some of the decorative icing tricks you taught me," I said, pointing to some of the flowers I'd created.

"So, when I cut into this, there's a molten chocolate center. Is that right?" Betsy asked.

"Yes, the original recipe from your Aunt Ellie and my grandma didn't have a liquid chocolate center. I modernized it. You can ask your customers that are eating in if they'd like it heated but warn them to be careful as that will make the inside filling hot. Some ice cream would be delicious with it. Maybe anyone taking some home, give them a heads up what's inside. But people can eat it without warming it up too."

"Man, Aunt Ellie would have been so proud to know how well the store she left to me is doing and seeing you and Ava take her and her BFF's recipes and modernizing them and using them in your restaurant and in cross-selling around the town." A few tears fell down her cheek and she wiped them away quickly.

Betsy's Aunt Ellie was my grandma's best friend growing up. Then Ellie was murdered and grandma became the prime suspect. That's how Ava and I got started with the investigative business. Betsy had been a nurse back then, but Ellie left her niece her chocolate shop since she had no children of her own.

I noticed Betsy's attention had drifted back to the window and I looked out, seeing Tabitha and Teddy go from talking to hugging. Betsy looked troubled at the sight of them together. She and Teddy had always been great friends but both of them showed signs of feeling something more for each other.

I wondered if part of Tabitha's undercover work tied into a fake relationship with Teddy for some reason. I'd never thought those two seemed like a good romantic fit and it was very obvious Teddy was in love with Betsy even if Betsy was oblivious to it.

"That's right, you and Teddy have always been close friends. You probably know his dad as well as anyone from high school, right?"

I proceeded to repeat the contradictory rumors I'd heard about Harvey as Betsy nodded.

"Yeah, I've heard all the rumors too. From what I know, it's one of those things where you're a kid and your parents have this whole other life that you know nothing about. You know what I mean?"

I'm not sure the look I had on my face, but Betsy recognized it to mean I didn't understand.

"I'm not necessarily talking about anything nefarious or a secret life. Well, maybe." She shrugged her shoulders, looking at the ceiling momentarily. "I just mean Teddy heard all the rumors too and tried to talk to his dad about it. Harvey gave him some blanket parental statement like, *Son, people in small towns love to gab, don'tcha worry about it. You know who your old dad is.*"

"Oh, yeah, I know all about that." I thought about the catastrophe that is my family. Two uncles at each other's throats. Secret love children. Lies. Deception. Drama.

"Yeah, even though Teddy and Tabitha are an item now, he and I are still friends. He hasn't been himself lately. Something is going on but I don't know if it's his dad or not. That's why I was hoping to talk to him." She looked down at her feet. "I'm sorry, do you want a snack or something to drink?"

"A cup of any tea you have is great, thanks. Am I keeping you from something pressing?"

"Not at all. There's a lull right now. I'll join you," she said, bringing the large white electric kettle over with an assortment of flavors of teabags to choose from.

I chose coconut chai, dipped it into my hot water in the mug, added some sweetener and cream and allowed it to steep. "Have you heard anything from Lydia?"

"Yes, she's been texting pictures of her and baby Monty at the beach. She really needed this vacation," Betsy said, stirring her chamomile tea.

"But is she enjoying it with Lory and Karl?" I asked. Last winter, the holiday season was filled with family dysfunction here in Leavensport but none came close to what poor Lydia experienced with her mom and dad. If any family deserved a vacation, it was them.

"Um, depends on the hour. Sometimes I get pictures with them and everyone looks happy enough. Other times she is sending me GIFS of cartoon girls losing their minds as their parents fight behind them." Betsy laughed.

"Wow, she and I have so much in common," I said, sipping my tea.

"Well, they're all trying. Lydia did tell me that Karl said he and Lory wanted to try and be better grandparents to Monty than they were parents to Lydia."

"That is something, alright," I said as a customer walked into the bakery.

It was the new high school principal, Bobby Zane, who was all smiles today with Betsy. That guy made my skin crawl. He came off as a real shyster. Although, I may be biased since I saw him with Caleb and Asher the other night.

"I'll have my usual. Boy, your smile really lights up a room," he said to Betsy. He turned to me with the same hundred-watt smile until he realized who I was. Then it faded.

"Hi, Bobby." I attempted my best upbeat tone.

His voice melted from cheery to leery in seconds. "Oh, hello." He turned back to Betsy. "Thanks, doll, I'm hoping to make it back after lunch today for some dessert. Hopefully, I'll be able to eat in and we can chat—alone." He looked jeeringly over at me as he swung the door open, then pasted his best smile back on for Betsy's benefit.

"Seems like someone has a crush. You must be a real catch, Betsy. Teddy, Bradley, and now this guy," I teased her, enjoying watching her cheeks flush.

Waving a hand at me, Betsy said, "Oh, you, stop that! He seems nice enough. He asked me to chaperone this year's prom. I think he's being overly nice out of desperation for volunteers."

"Not true, he doesn't seem to like me too much and Ava and I are volunteering." I sipped more tea.

"Really, are you doing it? I will do it if I know you both will be there! It'll be fun!"

"Yes, we're going to do it. Although, come to think of it, I was supposed to ask Ava but I already committed her to do it. I guess I should tell her."

Betsy's cackle echoed against the walls in the small bakery. "I'd love to be a fly on the wall when you tell her."

I parked my Honda in front of the library and ran a few books I'd checked out inside. I was heading back to my car when I heard someone yelling, "Hey, Josie—JOSIE WAIT UP!!!"

I pulled on the handle of my car door until I realized the voice was drawing nearer to me. I looked up to see the Italian supermodel, Imelda, waving me down. I couldn't help an eye roll at her getting my name wrong.

"It's Jo-LEE," I enunciated. "Not Jo-SEE."

"Oh, sorry about that," she said unapologetically.

I stared awkwardly at her for what felt like ten minutes. "What did you need?" I finally asked.

"I wanted to see if you'd be uncomfortable with me asking Mick out for dinner while I'm in town." She stared down at her well-manicured hand then flicked her eyes up without moving her head.

Would I be uncomfortable? Uncomfortable? Um, YES! You tall, lanky—

"I mean, no. Why would I be uncomfortable?"

"You just seemed—so, what's the word? Per—perplexing the other day."

Perplexing? Me? Witch don't even—

"I don't understand," I said, looking around for a way to leave this conversation. Of course, no one I knew was out walking during this gorgeous spring afternoon.

"Exactly," Imelda spat out. "Oh, awkward, that was the word I meant. You are awkward." She towered over me, smoothing out her long, thick locks then flipping them over her shoulder.

I half-expected her to challenge me to a walk-off right in the middle of Leavensport. "Awkward? I'm not awkward." I finally worked up the courage to say what I thought—even if she was right.

"Sorry, my English is not great. I didn't mean to be so antagonistic—I have been told that since I've been doing my Krav Maga training, I have been more aggressive."

So, you can use the word antagonistic perfectly, but you struggle with the English language. Okay, you catty little—

"No worries, I completely understand." I laid a hand on her forearm with my most sugary fake voice and grinned at her as if I felt sorry for her.

Imelda's eyes narrowed.

"I worry you don't understand the type of family you married into," Imelda said out of the blue.

She knew exactly the game she was playing. I was tempted to blurt it all out but I knew that she was an old family friend and Lord knows that the Milano family is not thrilled with me. Oh, screw it!

"I know EXACTLY the kind of man I married. That's all I need to know." I crossed my arms, hoping it came across as haughty and not pouty. Who did she think she was anyway? I knew exactly what the Milano family was and so did Mick. It's why he changed his last name and became a cop. As connected as he was to his family, he didn't agree with their choices and lifestyle. I hated who they were as much as Mick and found it odd that his family never brought it up. Mick and I talked about it a lot and I know it's something he worked on in therapy.

"This is a different situation than your typical family," Imelda said.

"Aren't you bringing some oil here or something? You know, we found some oil caps in a field near Mick's restaurant a few months back. I don't suppose you know anything about that, do you?"

"I don't. Finding buried secrets. Seems dangerous." Imelda took one step forward, staring me straight in the eye.

I took an uncomfortable step forward, not wanting to back down and said, "You know, back to your original question about having dinner with MY husband, no, I don't mind at all. Old pals and all that." I smiled sweetly and got in my car and drove off before she could utter another word.

I finally made it to Cast Iron Creations and was carrying in Betsy's desserts when I heard my actual name being called out.

"Jolie, it's Nina, I've got the door," she said, running in front of me and opening the door with one hand, balancing a big white cardboard box in the other.

"Oh, thank you!" I moved to the counter and put the bag of raspberry chocolate cakes down.

"Sure thing! I decided to join in the cross-selling and brought over some sugar cookies decorated with spring flowers, bees, birds, and trees with buttercream icing." She handed the box over the counter.

I opened it to see piles and piles of delicious-looking, beautifully decorated white-and-yellow daisies and black-and-yellow bumble bees. "Gorgeous! You have real talent! What price would you like me to put on these? Did you bring a sign or business cards so I can make sure everyone knows they are yours and where to find you?"

"Oh, sorry, I didn't think about any of that." She reached in her pocket. "I do have a few business cards though. Here you go."

"Great, I'll put one up on the business board over there and put these by your cookies. I'll display them and make a sign. I'll text you how much we sold and I can send your money through PayPal."

A thought flittered in my mind and I couldn't help but ask. "Do you know a cookie's favorite time of day?"

Nina stood still and rolled her eyes around speculatively. "Um, no?"

"Crunch time!" I laughed so loud that Bea Seevers, who was eating at a nearby table, looked up from her soup and grinned, shook her head then continued slurping.

Crickets.

"Oh, good one." Nina grinned half-heartedly, then changed the subject. "Also, I wanted to thank you for calling me the other night and letting me know about Luis. I really appreciate it."

"No problem at all," I said as I noticed Bea getting up and moving toward the box of cookies.

"Those look delicious. I'd love two for dessert and can I buy six to go?"

"Of course!" I said.

Ava came from the kitchen, hearing the end of the conversation, and picked up a small Styrofoam box big enough to hold half a dozen cookies. She found some tongs and began picking out six cookies and said to Nina, "You know, I still can't believe you lived in Santo Domingo and you aren't related to or don't know the Sanchez family. I mean, I thought everyone had at least heard of them."

"Well, I haven't. I mean, only my mom and dad in Santo Domingo but I'm not that close to anyone else in my family," Nina spat out quickly and looked away.

"So, you are from Santo Domingo, then!" Ava declared in a *gotcha* kind of way.

Nina's head jerked back momentarily as her eyes moved around. "Yes, I am, but I don't know of a big Sanchez family from there."

"Jolie, don't you think her son, Luis, looks a lot like Theo?" Ava asked me, referring to her sister's husband, Theo Sanchez.

My mouth dropped open slightly. "I kept thinking he looked like a celebrity but that's it. He does!"

"I have no clue what either of you are talking about," Nina hissed. She turned haughtily on her heel and stormed out.

"Wow, I thought she was starting to warm up to us for a hot minute," I said.

"I don't trust her," Ava said.

"She's kind of rude, and the cookies are good but way overpriced," Bea said.

"Hey, can I ask you something?" I asked Bea as Ava grabbed the decaf coffee pot when she saw a couple locals raise their cups in the air.

"What's up, doll?"

"Did you ever know Mr. Costello to be involved in criminal activities back in the nineties?"

"You're still investigating all that, child? Well, let's see, not that I can remember. I do remember that he and Harvey used to be the best of friends. Those two and Earl hung out all the time and I guess it was in the late nineties when it all blew up." Bea reached for her soft drink from the table she had been sitting at with her husband who had gotten up, paid, and headed out for a paper once he saw his wife was gabbing.

"What blew up?" I asked.

"I don't completely remember and of course that hubby of mine has up and taken off. Something that Harvey found out. But then Harvey left the job and left town in a hurry. I just remember that things weren't the same with Earl and Tom after that."

"Really, I've never thought they didn't get along," I said.

"Oh, you know men. They can punch each other and be fine the next day. They are fine, dear, it's just that they haven't been close since then."

"Do you know the truth about why Harvey left town?" I asked.

Mrs. Seevers looked like she was miles and miles away. "You know, I only remember that after he left Earl said something to me that still makes me shiver today."

"What's that?" I wondered out loud.

"He asked, *Do we ever really know who our neighbors are?*"

Chapter Eight

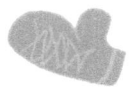

The next day, I was headed to Ralph & Stella's New York Pizza Pie to grovel at Stella's feet. On the way, I was on the phone with Tabitha, checking on her and doing a smidge of snooping.

"I was calling to check in and see how you're doing," I said, opening the sunroof to enjoy some fresh air as I drove.

"Better today, thanks," Tabitha started. "I'm sorry about the other night. Everything was still fresh and raw."

"Trust me, you never need to apologize to me for getting emotional. Not as many times as you've witnessed me in shambles."

"That's part of my job, though," Tabitha said, then asked me to hold on while she spoke to her receptionist. "Sorry about that, I'm back."

"No worries, I'm getting ready to meet someone. I wanted to ask you quickly. Are you and Teddy really a couple, or is that part of what you're doing undercover?"

"Why do you want to know that?" Tabitha asked.

"I saw you two talking yesterday. I don't know. I've never really understood your dating relationship." I didn't know how to explain it.

"Huh, I guess I'm not as good undercover as I thought," Tabitha said.

"Or I'm a dang good PI," I said. "Hey, gotta run."

I threw my phone in my tote, then pushed the door open to Ralph & Stella's New York Pizza Pie, taking in the welcoming, greasy, cheesy-spicy smells of New York pizza. Ralph had an unfortunate fate last fall and left his shop to Stella, who had worked for him. She'd kept his name in the business name to honor him.

"Hey, Jolie," Keith said to me as I walked toward the counter.

I could see he was with someone but couldn't tell who it was from the back of her head. "Hey, Keith, is Stella in the back?"

"She just took our order." Marissa turned around in her seat, looking me up and down like she was sizing me up.

"Oh." I took a noticeable gulp of nothing, feeling like a huge knot just traveled down my throat. "Marissa. You two are—" I stumbled for the right word.

"Did you place a to-go order?" Stella walked from the back around the counter.

"Um, no, I do need to talk to you, though." I pointed an index finger straight up, signaling I'd be there in just a minute, then turned to Marissa, wishing I could drum up more barf to spew on her as I finished my sentence, "—together."

"Yes, we're having lunch together. Can't get anything past you." Marissa gave Keith a *wow-she-*

is-a-real-moron look, then laughed half-heartedly.

"Awesome." I ignored her and moved toward Stella.

"You meeting Ava here?" Stella asked, avoiding eye contact with me and holding a pen and order pad, waiting.

"I'm not. Um, can I get two cheese slices to go please?" I hadn't planned on eating but that never stopped me before. Also, I felt weird with apologies. Like everyone loved them.

"Give me a few to get it together," Stella said, attempting to sprint away from me.

I grabbed her arm. "Hey, I was a total jerk at the meeting insinuating you shared a recipe with Marissa. I'm so sorry. I've been fighting the stomach flu, but that's not an excuse. There is none. I don't know what else to say."

There was a pause that felt like infinity, then Stella grinned.

"What's so funny?"

"It's hard for me to question if you are sick or not seeing that you puked all over Marissa." She fell over, laughing harder. "Only you and Ava—you two are too much."

I grinned impishly. "Yeah, I mean, still, no excuse. I really am sorry."

"I know. You already apologized. I accepted. Don't worry about it, we all have our days. We're friends. All is good. Thank you for another apology, though. I'm going to get your pizza. Be right back."

"Well, look at you!"

I turned to see Harvey Tobias standing eye-to-eye with me. He stood about two feet away from me but almost reached me with his jolly belly done up in a brown short-sleeved button-up shirt with navy suspenders holding his saggy jeans up. It looked like Mr. Tobias' hairline was starting to recede.

I reached out to hug him. "Hey, stranger. Long time no see."

"I know, a guy leaves for a few years and everyone goes and grows up on me. Look at my son the town chief now." He held out a short chubby hand to Teddy, who waved listlessly.

"He's doing great work." I gave Teddy a bit of friendly support.

"I hear you're married now, to that detective from Tri-City. I hope he doesn't follow in his brother's footsteps." Harvey's shiny grin was shadowed with concern.

"Which brother?" I asked wondering if he meant the one in prison or the previous mayor of Tri-City.

"Doesn't matter either way," Harvey said, beginning to say something else before Stella came out with my pizza.

I glanced at Stella and then turned back toward to Mr. Tobias, who had already rejoined the conversation with his son at their table.

I began digging around in my tote, trying to locate my wallet to pay and Stella noticed there was a crack in the box and grease was leaking out. "Oh, no. Hold on. I'm out of boxes up here. Give me just a minute to run back and get some from the storage closet."

"No rush," I said, thinking I needed some time to find my wallet anyway.

I pulled my wallet out, not realizing the zipper with all my change was open until it spilled out on the floor. I got down to retrieve the quarters and dimes first.

Crawling under a nearby table, I heard snatches of Teddy and Harvey's conversation. I pushed some coins closer to their table and crawled closer to them for better snooping position.

"Denise's ex-husband, Darrell, was one of the two men on the video from the murder scene," Teddy muttered.

Darrell?

After I left the pizza shop, I went to talk to Betsy at Chocolate Capers for the second day in a row.

"You just can't get enough chocolate, can you?" Betsy laughed as I walked in.

"Never," I replied without thought. I took a seat in the back by the fish tank while Betsy finished up with a line of customers getting chocolaty nibbles for later.

Betsy carried a pot of tea and a half-dozen double chocolate chunk and peanut butter cookies to the table. "What's up?"

"I just overheard Teddy tell his dad that Darrell was one of the two men on the security tape at the shelter for the unhoused residents. Did Teddy tell you who the other man was?" I shoved half of a cookie in my mouth.

"I called him last night, but Tabitha answered so I hung up." She looked up with flushed cheeks at me. "I know, it's childish. I was shocked. It's dumb."

I had just tried to take a sip of my hot tea but got more blistering hot liquid than I wanted and when Betsy mentioned Teddy and Tabitha, I gulped without thinking.

I wheezed loudly as scorching pain hit my trachea. I hacked a few times as uncontrollable tears squirted from my eyes.

"Are you okay?" Betsy started to get up but I used a hand to halt her.

"I'm okay," I mustered in a breathless whisper. "Sorry, I swallowed wrong. Give me a minute."

"I'll be right back." Betsy got up to help a new customer that walked inside.

I got up and moved to the water fountain near the restrooms and took a drink. Soothing. I hated knowing about Teddy and Tabitha. I wanted to tell Betsy. I knew I couldn't until I understood more of what was going on.

"What up?" Bradley said with a bag of fresh chocolate donuts in his hand that he had just purchased.

"Nothing and everything," I said grinning at Bradley, who was Leavensport's main reporter and one of my closest friends that grew up here.

"I hear that." He pulled over a chair from the table beside mine and sat down.

I looked up to see Betsy was taking a call. "How's Gemma doing?" I inquired about his latest love interest. She lived in Tri-City and ran Gemma's Bohemian Jewelry Store that connected to her best friend's shop Peggy's Pies and Purses. Ava and I had become great friends with the two women who were proving to be darn good investigators in the city. Not that they pursued a license like Ava and I did, but they'd helped us with city info on many occasions.

"Great, her business is booming right now," Bradley said. "She comes out with a new line of jewelry at the beginning of each season and I guess those are her busiest times of the year other than holiday gift-buying seasons."

I grinned at his knowing this information. He must really be into her. I was happy to finally see him settle into a relationship with someone who loved him equally. "I don't suppose you'd be willing to see if she could find out who the mayor of Tri-City was in 1997 and if she and Peggy could dig to find out if the mayor was into anything crime related or if there are any rumors on that person?"

"Well, I can tell you who the mayor was then. I've had to do political historical stories, but you can look it up quickly." Bradley held up his phone that had the name of the mayor of Tri-City in 1997.

"Yeah well, not everyone knows the best sites to use to find information off the top of their head like you—" I paused to inhale a sharp breath when I saw the name on Bradley's phone. "Noah Morrison!" I bellowed.

"The one and only," Bradley sneered. Noah was a man that people in Leavensport did not hold in high regard after last fall's fiasco. "I just did a quick search on Factcheck.org and found out that a lot of gentrification began with Morrison."

"Really! Okay," I said. I looked over and saw that Betsy had gotten off the phone, waited on a couple more customers and was heading back to my table.

"I have to take off. I have a meeting for an article." Bradley reached over and gave me a hug, then Betsy, and then he left.

"I just got a call from my supplier and they said my order is going to be two weeks late—which sucks, seeing that the special chocolate I order from Italy already takes so long to ship here."

"That sucks. Can you use some things from local stores in the meantime?"

"I can, but I charge a bit more because of how good the Amadei Tuscany chocolate is and people are willing to pay. Maybe I'll alter my prices and run it as a sale until it comes in. Anyway, I've been dying to know how you are enjoying your new home."

"Still unpacking and I keep moving furniture around trying to figure out how to best organize everything. It's so crazy, Betsy, this house is three times bigger than my previous cottage but putting all of our stuff together and all the cats—it's like how is this not enough room?" I held my hands up in despair.

Betsy laughed. "This is the kind of conversation that middle-aged people have. When did we get to be middle-aged?"

"We aren't, yet, but we'll be prepared! Not to mention, I've been fighting this stupid stomach bug that's going around town. It's like I'm sick one day and feel great the next or it's hour to hour."

"Maybe you need to go to the doctor," Betsy said, concerned.

"Every time I think of making an appointment, I'm feeling better." I shrugged my shoulders and took another sip of tea.

"When Aunt Ellie passed away, she left most of her stuff to me. I've struggled to part with it and now I'm in the same boat as you with all this—stuff!" She held out her arms as if she had a load full of junk.

"Maybe we should create a community-wide yard sale in July!"

"Oh perfect, you tell Mayor Nalini that. He will

just LOVE having another official Leavensport day to celebrate and mark as our own." Betsy giggled.

"True, that's the best way to make sure it happens. I know one of the first things I'll put in the sale and it's already in a huge bag ready to go."

Betsy tilted her head. "What's that?"

"This huge stupid green army surplus bag of men's shoes all in one size." I grinned.

Betsy looked quizzically at me.

"I was going through stuff unpacking the other night when I saw this bag I'd never seen before laying in the corner. It was this huge bag of shoes from lots of different decades. All one size. The size my husband wears." I put my head on my hands leaning toward Betsy knowingly.

"Oh my gosh, does Mick have more shoes than you do?"

I nodded, grinning. "He does. And you better bet when he got home that night, I made a point of teasing him about it. I asked him if we should build a he/she closet but make it an add-on room to the house. He looked at me like I was insane. Then I said, 'you know, for your gigantic bag of shoes.'"

"What did he say?"

"Oh, that is the best part of this story. He was so serious. He told me that if there is ever a global disaster and we survive to wander around the earth, it's important to have shoes."

"Wait, what?" Betsy looked at me waiting for me to say I was kidding. "No."

I shook my head. "That's what made it so funny is that he was serious."

We both started laughing hysterically.

"Oh my gosh, Jolie. You two are SO perfect for

each other!"

I stopped mid-laugh. "Huh? I don't have an army bag full of shoes for when the world is about to end."

"No, I know, but you are so obsessive-compulsive about some things. He's just like you in some ways. You know what I mean." Her cell rang and she held up a finger as she answered.

I thought to myself, *No, I don't know what you mean. I'm not that weird. Am I?* I looked up as Betsy clicked her phone.

"You have an odd look on your face," I said, noticing Betsy's coy smile as her green eyes lit up.

"Yeah, I think I found a way to move on from Teddy."

"Oh, really?" I fussed with the napkin and silverware on the table, feeling antsy at what I knew.

"I was just asked out on a date and I accepted," Betsy said.

"With who?"

"Bobby, the new principal." Betsy smiled sheepishly.

I had a bad feeling about this, but it passed as my cell rang. It was Mick. I looked at Betsy and said, "Speak of the devil."

"Hey baby, we were just talking about you. I was telling Betsy—"

Mick cut me off with a serious tone. "Jolie, Mary's in labor and I'm on my way to arrest Carlos."

Chapter Nine

I parked the Honda in the closest spot I could find at the Pine Valley hospital lot, shouldered my tote, and sprinted toward the doors. I heard my name being yelled and stopped and turned.

Mick was running after me. "Hey, sorry, force of habit," he said, putting an arm around me and kissing me.

"Why are you arresting Carlos?" I couldn't help but ask immediately after kissing him back.

"You know I can't say anything to you at this point." He looked hard at me.

I nodded and pulled my cell from my jeans pocket and dialed the Leavensport lawyer realizing he should share part of his retainer with me for all the business I throw his way. "Hi Mr. Mecurio, this is Jolie Tucker, again. As you know, Carlos Hernandez is our employee. He is at Pine Valley hospital and about to be taken into police custody. I'd like you to represent him. I'll take care of the cost. Can you meet him at the police station now, please?" I looked up at Mick, who nodded in agreement to what I was doing. I hung up and sighed.

"Well, when we walk through those doors, you do what you need to do and I will do what I need to do but we'll meet up at home later, regardless." He bent down to kiss me again.

I reached up around him and hugged him tightly, feeling tears spring to my eyes. "I hate being on the opposite side of you."

"Me too, baby. Me too." He pulled back and we shared one last look, then he took off through the revolving door.

I waited a minute or two to allow Mick to get an elevator before me. I didn't want us walking in together and have anyone think he wasn't doing his job the right way.

When I got up to the delivery floor, Carlos had already been taken in to be with Mary while she gave birth.

"Please let him have time to see his baby be born," I said, putting an arm on Mick's arm.

"You know I can't do that." He pulled out his badge and went to the head nurse.

I stayed in the waiting area after letting someone behind a desk know who I was and who I was here for. They informed me that Mirabelle was sitting by a TV set with Spy sitting faithfully next to her. She was rubbing long strides down his furry golden back as he sat watching the cartoon with her.

"Hey lady," I said.

Mirabelle turned around and squealed, "JOLIE! I'm getting a baby brother!"

"I know you are! This is SO exciting!" I put as much enthusiasm in my voice as I could muster on Mirabelle's behalf. She was Mary's twenty-something-year-old daughter with Down Syndrome who had sight issues and a seeing-eye dog named Spy. She was also Cast Iron Creations' best hostess ever.

"My mom is going to call him Georges, I think." Mirabelle started then startled me by yelling, "Carlos! No! You can't leave now. Mommy needs you."

I turned as she got up and ran to her stepfather with Spy right by her side.

"It's Jorge, precious girl." Carlos helped Mirabelle pronounce his son's name after overhearing while his hands were cuffed behind his back. Mick stood near him, holding one of his elbows.

I noticed Mick had taken a blanket from a nearby cart and placed it over the cuffs on Carlos' hands, and moved from holding his arm to putting a friendly arm around him for Mirabelle's sake. I knew he was only doing his job and I knew it was killing him to do it. He liked Carlos and he loved Mirabelle as much as everyone in Leavensport did.

"But why are you here? Did Mommy have my brother already?" She looked from Carlos to Mick and gave Mick a huge smile. "Hi, Mick!" She hugged him.

I saw my husband wince. "Hello, beautiful!" I could tell he was trying to keep his voice from cracking.

"I need your stepdad to come with me and help me on a case right now, Mirabelle," Mick said.

Carlos nodded in agreement. "That's right. It's real important, otherwise you know I'd never go."

Okay, I wasn't going to be able to be strong much longer and I wanted to blurt out *What on earth is going on here anyways?* But I kept my mouth shut and swallowed my emotions. I saw Ava and Delilah walking toward us and waved them over.

"Um, should I be with Mommy?" Mirabelle looked worried.

"No sweetie, you can stay with me," Delilah said, putting a reassuring hand on her shoulder.

Spy was whining sitting next to Mirabelle feeling everyone's tension.

"She's got Jolie's grandma and aunt in there with her," Carlos said, nodding and smiling at Mirabelle.

"I didn't know they were here?" I questioned the group.

"I called them before I called you," Mick said looking at me wistfully.

As Delilah took Mirabelle and Spy back to the TV in the waiting area, Ava said, "I'm texting them to see if I can come back and give them a break."

Mick started to take Carlos out but not before I cut him off. "I called a lawyer. They are meeting you at the station. I know he's your friend," I nodded toward Mick, "but don't say anything at all—nothing. Don't even be friendly. Just be quiet until you see Mr. Mercurio at the station."

"I can't afford—" Carlos started.

"Don't worry about it. I'll take care of it," I said.

"But no—" Carlos protested.

"She has her own checking account. It won't be a conflict of interest," Mick whispered.

"It's not that. She's done too much for me. I don't know when I could pay you back," Carlos pleaded with me.

"I don't care. Just please do not say anything.

He likes you, but he has to do his job. So, no matter what he says, do not speak to him, Teddy, Keith, no one from this point on except Mr. Mecurio. Got it?"

Carlos nodded as Mick nodded at me and pushed Carlos toward the elevator.

I looked around. Ava must have gone back to be with Mary and my family and Delilah was watching over Mirabelle. Mirabelle loved Delilah. Delilah had done some art therapy with Mirabelle for the past several years and she was turning into quite the budding artist.

Bea Seevers came trotting in before I could return to Delilah and Mirabelle. "Jolie, how is she? Is Carlos with her? Does he know?"

I bit my lower lip. "Ava's in there with her now. Mick just arrested Carlos but I'm not sure why. I wasn't around when he read the charges."

"What? That's horrible!" Mrs. Seevers declared.

Before she could ask me a hundred more questions, my family came bumbling towards us from down the hall. "What on earth is that son-in-law of mine think he is doing?" My Grandma Opal added a curt ending to each syllable. I knew that was never a good sign.

"Grandma, he's doing his job. He doesn't like it, either," I said, using my hands to signal her to be quiet, then pointed to Mirabelle.

"How is she doing?" Aunt Fern asked. She loved Mirabelle so much. She always called her our hostess-with-the-mostess which always made Mirabelle giggle.

"She was here when Mick took Carlos, but they hid what was really going on, so she doesn't know," I said seeing my mom come running down the hall. I filled her in quickly on what we knew so far.

"Well, we can—" my grandma started then stopped, staring behind me, slack-jawed.

I turned around to see my best friend standing there, her eyes as wide as I'd ever seen them. She looked to be in a daze and her beautiful adobe skin had gone pale.

"Ava." I moved toward her.

"Mary had Jorge, but—" Ava started and looked around for Mirabelle.

"She's with Delilah over there." I pointed seeing Delilah get up to move toward our group.

Ava's head bobbed up and down automatically, then she finished her sentence. "But Mary, she's, well, she lost a lot of blood. They took her off for emergency surgery. I heard a doctor telling a nurse to have Mary ready to go in less than two minutes. He wasn't sure if she'd make it."

All six of us women stood as still as trees for several moments allowing the realization of what Ava had just said to sink in. I looked over toward Delilah and thought about Carlos. I swallowed hard. Then I shook myself out of it.

"Okay, Mirabelle cannot know this yet," I said, biting a fingernail. "Aunt Fern, you call Converge Life and Faith Church and talk to every clergy person there, putting Mary on a list for good thoughts, prayers, and vibes. Mom, you go be with Mirabelle while Ava explains everything going on to Delilah. We need to figure out what to do with Mirabelle during all this and what to tell her."

"First off, she'll stay with us," Ava said firmly.

Wow, my bestie was going to make a wonderful mother.

"Delilah probably has the strongest relationship with her outside of Carlos and Mary,"

Ava said. "She'll know how to best take care of her."

"And me and my girls will take Carlos' shifts at the restaurant," my grandma said as my aunt and mom nodded in agreement.

"We can also help watch Mirabelle and be with Mary when Delilah can't be with her or when you girls need help," my mom said.

"Count me in that too," Bea said.

Bea startled me as I turned around. I had forgotten she was there. She normally wasn't so silent.

As much as my family and the people in this small town could drive me batty, this is exactly why I loved living here. When life got tough, we all rallied around each other.

My mom went to be with Mirabelle while Ava explained what was going on to Delilah and Aunt Fern was off making her phone calls to summon the angels to watch over Mary.

"They said she wants the baby's name to be Jorge," I told my grandma, who sat next to me. I put my head on her shoulder as she reached an arm up to smooth my hair.

"That's after Carlos' great grandfather," Grandma said.

"How'd you know that?" I pulled back from her shoulder, looking into her dark Cherokee eyes.

"Carlos and I talked at the restaurant one evening when things were slow. We got to talking about recipes and he told me about his family in Mexico. I told him about your grandpa's ancestors who came from the hills of Kentucky and my family's tribe from West Virginia."

"Wow, that's nice," I said. "I didn't know they were naming the child after his great-grandfather. I bet he would have loved to be here for that."

"He's hoping to get them here to meet Jorge," Grandma said. "He's doing everything he can."

"Wait, did he tell you what's going on?" I asked carefully.

"I don't know what you're talking about," Grandma said.

"Okay." I didn't believe her, but I knew that with Mary in the hospital fighting for her life, Carlos facing jail time for who knows what, and Mirabelle's happiness at stake, Ava and I needed to get to the bottom of Janelle's death ASAP!

It had been a long night at the hospital and Mary had made it out of surgery, but when I left at two in the morning, she hadn't gained consciousness. Aunt Fern took Grandma home so she could sleep in her own bed, then she went home to get some rest so she could open the restaurant this morning. Delilah felt strongly that we needed to be honest with Mirabelle. If she found out from someone else, it could be a lot worse later. She and Ava took Mirabelle and Spy to their house to break the news to her there.

I was at Kwani's Fillin Station filling up my gas tank before running to the bank. I finished pumping the gas, headed into the station to get a Big Gulp and pay when I saw Tom Costello, Grandma Opal, and Aunt Fern in a heated argument in front of the ice machine.

My grandma looked shaken. I walked up in front of Aunt Fern, who had just finished giving Tom a piece of her mind, "—absolutely disgusting. You should be ASHAMED of yourself." She pointed a bony finger at him.

"Fernie." My grandma reached for her daughter's arm, but Aunt Fern jerked away from her.

"Bea Seevers is married. Good Lord, what are you thinking, man?" Aunt Fern raised her large, heavy, rhinestone-studded white faux leather purse over her head to get more leverage, then took a strong swing at Tom's head.

I made the mistake of stepping in the middle of the two of them. Before I realized what was happening, I felt a scratch on my forehead as the large white shark of a purse scraped along my head then smacked me square in the cheek. I felt some liquid rush from somewhere on my head as I felt the sting of what a rhinestone stud felt like. My body jerked in rhythm with my head and did a partial spin into Mr. Costello, who helped me keep my footing.

"OH, are you okay?" My grandma ran to me and took my face in her hands, looking me over, then saying, "It looks okay, honey. You'll have a mark on your cheek and you got a little scrape that caught you right smack in the center of your forehead, but you'll live."

"LOOK WHAT YOU MADE ME DO TO MY NIECE!" Aunt Fern screeched at Tom, who looked helplessly from the ground to Grandma to me to the ground again, then he turned away, slumped shouldered, and drug his feet off slowly.

I kind of felt sorry for him, then I remembered what I heard Aunt Fern say. "Did he and Mrs. Seevers have an affair?" I asked, aghast.

"No, good Lord, she has enough sense not to do that," my grandma said.

"Margie told me he was hanging all over her

last night at M&M's restaurant. He was hitting the hooch at the bar and she had to ask him to leave, when he started putting the moves on her," Aunt Fern said.

"Ew, gross," I said, then looked at my grandma, who looked devastated.

"I guess he's moved on," she said.

"You go on home," I said to Aunt Fern. "I'll take Grandma home."

Aunt Fern nodded, bent down to kiss Grandma on the cheek, lightly kissed the booboo she made on my head, then gently leaned her head against me and whispered, "Sorry I clocked you, sista."

I grinned and slapped goofily at her.

"Grandma, I have to go pay for my gas," I said. "Let's get a cup of tea and sit in the back for a minute." I put a hand on her lower back to lead her inside Kwani's.

"It's a good thing you used to live so close and I saw you so often or I'd think you were trying to steal gas from me," Kwani, the owner, said with a jolly smile.

Ava and Delilah still lived close to his shop, but my place now belonged to Marissa, I thought indignantly to myself.

Grandma and I got to-go cups and I got a Big Gulp Blue Raspberry Slurpee while Grandma got a large coffee.

"You're going to have a blue tongue," Grandma said.

I grinned. For as long as I could remember, I loved anything that gave me a blue tongue and my grandma loved to give me grief over it.

"You have never told me what really happened

with you and Tom. Don't you think it's time?"

Grandma Opal chewed her coffee stirrer. "There were so many rumors about him back in the nineties. I'd heard some back then but didn't think much of it. Bea told me that Tom had cheated on his late wife, Wanda, back in the day. I never knew that."

"Oh, wow. I mean, I can see why that would create trust issues for you, but at the same time, he was a different age and a different man back then. Don't you think people can change?" I asked.

Grandma Opal shrugged her shoulders. "I thought about that, but then she told me who he slept with."

"Who?"

"Ellie." My grandma's eyes filled with tears.

I felt my purse-wounded cheek grow even sorer with anger. "Betsy's aunt. No WAY!"

"I can't really ask her now, can I?"

"Oh, Grandma, I wish I would have known what you were going through! Now I feel horrible thinking while you were miserable, I was up at the altar where you should have been with Tom but I was marrying Mick." Now tears were welling up in my eyes.

"Don't you dare feel bad. You did nothing wrong. I'm happy it all happened the way it did—well—other than not being there to witness it. Your happiness is the most important thing to me and your mom. You know that." She put that bulldog stern look back on her face then said, "Now, you get me home and get home to that hot detective of yours."

I grinned after dropping Grandma Opal off at her house. She went on and on about Mick the entire ride. I was happy she wasn't holding it against him about arresting Carlos anymore. At least she'd stopped flirting with him since we got married.

My cell rang and I pressed the button for Bluetooth. "Hello?"

"Hey, Jolie, it's Missy Smith. Just reminding you that the prom is this coming weekend. Could you and Ava be at the high school gym around six to help finish up decorations and set up the snack area?"

Oh crap! "Um, sure, of course," I said, pulling into a driveway to turn around.

I hung up from Missy and looked back to make sure no one was coming either way, then pulled out, turning around to head to Ava's house. I thought the stomach flu was coming back. I still hadn't told Ava about the chaperoning this weekend. This was not going to be fun.

I looked down as my phone buzzed again. What now? I thought. It was my mom.

"What's up, mom?"

"Jolie, I'm at the hospital with Mary."

I gulped.

Chapter Ten

"How's Mirabelle doing?" I asked as soon as Ava opened the door.

"She's in here with the girls, spoiling them is what she's doing," Ava said loudly.

"JOLIE," Mirabelle squeaked and ran to hug me.

"Hi sweetie, how are you?"

"I'm okay. I'm saying my prayers every night for Mommy." She put her head down making her bobbed dark blonde wisps hit her cheeks.

"Well," I said, grinning, "I just called *my* mommy and she's with *your* mom now at the hospital and I found out she's awake now!"

Mirabelle's face lit up. "Delilah, did you hear? Our prayers worked! They really worked! Mommy is awake. Spy, Mommy is awake!" Mirabelle ran to hug her companion, who woofed softly in her ear, then licked her cheek.

"Well, I'm getting my purse and taking us over so we can see her."

Delilah paused and looked at me and I picked up on the cue that she was questioning if Mary could have visitors or not. I nodded enthusiastically. I would never have told Mirabelle if she wasn't ready for visitors, but my mom said Mary was extremely stressed and kept calling out for Mirabelle. I knew it would help both of them to see each other.

All three black kittens were curled up in a fluffy rust-colored blanket and the forest-green couch. Mirabelle bent down to kiss Lily, Luna, and Lulu on the head before picking up the puppy dog bookbag Ava and I bought her for Christmas. She loved to look through my tote and had spent the last few months adding to her "big bag like Jolie has."

"Okay, we're heading out," Delilah said, kissing Ava.

"You aren't coming?" Mirabelle asked Ava.

"Nah, I got to stay here with Jolie and talk to her about something." Ava hugged Mirabelle.

"I can't believe you don't care if I go," I teased Mirabelle.

Mirabelle's thick glasses jiggled on her face as she laughed at me. "Anywhere Ava goes, you go."

"She has a point," Delilah said wryly, and they headed out with Spy following.

"I don't think Delilah is that thrilled with me right now," I said, plopping on the couch, which made the girls' fur puff out as they leaped to the ottoman, then scattered in three directions.

"Nice," Ava huffed.

"What? You terrorize my cats all the time. Payback. Plus, they love their Auntie Jolie."

Ava raised one eyebrow, giving me an icy look and crossing her arms. I swear if she were a cartoon character, she'd have steam spouting out of her ears.

"Calm down, this will all seem like nothing when I tell you why I really came here," I said, hoping to lighten the mood.

I was wrong.

"What did you do now?" Ava seemed genuinely frustrated.

I needed to rip off the bandage. "I told Missy Smith you and I would chaperone prom this year." I crossed my legs, uncrossed them, then crossed them again on the couch waiting for her to blow.

"Oh, okay," Ava shrugged casually then giggled. "I thought it was going to be something bad."

"Phew," I said dramatically wiping my brow. "For a minute there, I thought you were going to lose it. Yeah, I just got off the phone with Missy and she said if we can be there at six that would be great. It's this Saturday."

Ava had been moving to the kitchen to get us a beverage and I was following her. She got to the island as I finished my statement and held onto the stool tightly. Her body froze, then she bent over and I saw her shoulders jut up and down like she was dancing to a Billie Eilish song. I couldn't tell if she was laughing or crying. Then, it dawned on me that she was pregnant.

"Oh no, are you okay? Do you need me to call someone?" I took one long stride to her side.

Ava shook her head causing her thick, dark, curls to bounce around her face. "What are you talking about?" Ava turned her face to me and I saw tear-streaked raccoon eyes.

"What did I do? You were fine just a minute ago!"

"This Saturday? THIS Saturday—let me stress the THIS for the Jolie hour who needs everything explained to her in big all cap letters. Always with the Bambi eyes—oh look at me, I have no clue how inconsiderate I can be—yet I have to make everyone else think they are the problem," Ava said the words so fast it all sounded like one long blended word. Her voice was shaky and she took a huge deep breath and sat on the stool, bent over and put her head in her hands.

I stood very still, wondering whether I should be offended, agree with her and do more serious therapy, laugh, comfort her, or slowly back toward the door.

I chose comfort. "Hey, I'm sorry. I meant to tell you right after she asked but then everything happened, and I forgot until she just called. You're right. It was insensitive and you don't have to go. I didn't know you were pregnant then. You have a good excuse to not go!" I rubbed her back soothingly.

"But they can't know that!" she wailed, flailing her hands in the air.

"True, but I can tell them it's the stomach bug. It's been going around." I was starting to catch on to the hormonal waves now and trying to go with the flow of the mood. Also, I realized Delilah probably didn't hate me as much as I thought she did. She just needed to take out her aggression on someone. I could handle it.

I continued to rub Ava's back as she sniffed then she pulled her head up and side-eyed me like I was insane.

I stopped touching her and held my hand in the air, afraid to make a sudden move. My blue eyes darted left to right then to her wild eyes. I was nervous.

Ava let out an enormous, rank burp. I swore I could see green stench in the air and I tried to not look terrified. I held my breath hoping I wouldn't turn purple while still afraid to move.

Next, Ava's shoulders started gyrating again and I reached for a napkin to give her as she looked up, but this time she was cracking up, snorting, and trying not to fall off the stool.

I felt my muscles loosen as I grinned, then laughed. Ava reached out with tears in her eyes and held my hands and laughed maniacally. I felt like my gut would bust; I laughed so hard.

"Whew," Ava said, minutes later as I tried to stretch out my left side to loosen a pulled muscle from too much hard laughing.

"Okay, I'll go. I'll just need to lay down often," she said, pushing herself up to grab a couple of Coke Zeros.

"Sit down," I said.

"Huh?"

"Sit—you said 'lay' but you meant to say sit. It's preggo brain probably." I laughed.

Ava stood very still.

Oh no, what did I do? I tipped my head up, looking toward the heavens, then allowed it to flop forward, showing my despair.

Ava giggled again. "Gotcha!"

I scrunched up my nose. "BRAT!"

"Okay, well, maybe you, Mick, me, Delilah, and Tabitha should meet Saturday before our chaperoning duties," Ava said.

"Sounds good." I picked up my phone.

"What are you doing?"

"Texting all three of them now. Isn't it obvious?

I need to do it in the moment or I forget!"

Neon colors shined through the pillowy clouds as dusk settled on Leavensport. I stopped by the restaurant to check on my grandma and mom, who were taking the closing shift tonight.

"What are you doing here? Don't you know how to take a day off?" My mom asked while wiping down a table after collecting the dishes and piling them in the bin. She picked the bin of dirty dishes up and wrapped an arm around it, swinging the container on her hip as she followed me back to the kitchen.

"It's slow," I said, holding the swinging doors open for her.

"It wasn't earlier," I heard my grandma bellow from the sink where she was washing up some dishes.

Mom lugged a new set of dishes on the counter.

"It never ends," Grandma grumbled, putting the crusted dishes in first to soak and looking at what could go in the dishwasher. With cast iron, we had to be careful how we cleaned many of the kitchen items.

"It means business is good," my mom said cheerily.

Grandma and my mom were polar opposites. Mom was a true Pollyanna while Grandma was a negative Nelly. My biological father was a victim. I always wondered where that left me to be. I always wanted to avoid the extremes, but it seemed that it just made me end up being the truth-teller and no one liked that person. Luckily, Mick understood me. We'd discussed how he fits that mold, too, with his family.

I started helping to dry the dishes while mom prepped some things for breakfast tomorrow and started doing some closing chores in the kitchen. We had all gotten into a work groove when we heard the bell to the front door jingle.

In unison, we all looked to the front to see Tom Costello and Harvey Tobias walk inside, glaring at each other as the argument that had obviously started on the street moved in my dining area.

"Oh, come on, Harvey! You know I'd never do anything to screw you over on purpose!" Tom yelled.

"How do I know that? Who else knew those things? You think Earl would say something? There was only you, man." Harvey gave a little shove at Tom.

Tom began posturing and Grandma stumbled out front. "You two knock it off this instant!" All four foot eight inches of Grandma stood in between the towering men with her short, stubby finger pointing from one nose to the other and a bulldog look and screech that sent shivers down my spine.

Both men took a step back. It looked like Grandma had quickly diffused the situation.

I came out and picked up a coffee pot. "You two want a cup of decaf and so you can sit down to talk as adults?"

"Not decaf," Harvey said, pulling out a chair, turning it around, and straddling it like he was a cowboy in the Old West.

Men.

"Um, no, for you two, I'm going to choose decaf," I said, pulling a chair out for Tom and filling up two coffee cups.

Tom took the seat and sat hesitantly.

I took the chair in the middle of the two. "Now, what's the deal?"

Both men looked at me. Tom looked to be dry-washing his hands as Harvey swallowed hard then pinched his lips shut.

"No one wants to start? Okay, I will," I went on stubbornly. "I heard you two and Earl Seevers used to be the best of buds here in Leavensport," I started as both men's faces turned a shade of burgundy.

Tom shrugged. "Yeah, what's your point?"

"What's my point? Um, just that this is my restaurant that you two lugs burst into with your fighting. Luckily there are no customers now to witness your behavior," I scolded them. "So, I'll ask again. What gives?"

I admit to using this to my advantage. I was trying to find out some information.

"You always thought Earl was the nice guy of the group," Tom said, taking a drink of his coffee and deciding to add some sugar and creamer.

"Because he was," Harvey said.

"He's the one who told me you were trying to get a warrant to arrest me. I told you about the jam I was in with those hoods. I came to you in confidence for help. I was embarrassed. I had a wife and kids, Harvey. I was afraid for them. It wasn't like I wanted to allow them to use my basement to do their dirty business. Why would you turn it around on me?"

"I'd never—" Harvey started. "Earl told you that?"

Tom nodded with earnest eyes.

"Okay, I think I'm starting to follow here. But, Mr. Tobias, why did you really leave your job and the town?"

He looked stunned.

"I'm sorry. There are so many rumors flying around. I don't know if anyone knows if you were fired, told to stand down, or if you quit. I don't know!" I tilted my head.

"Fair enough," Harvey said, standing to turn the chair around and sit normally.

Grandma had gone back to help mom in the kitchen, but my spidey senses could *feel* them leaning in to hear this.

"Tom here went to the mayor and told him I was looking to jam him up. I always thought Mayor Richardson was involved. I wasn't trying to jam you up, Tom. I was trying to find out what was really going on in town." Harvey shook his head hard to show his disgust.

"How was I supposed to chance that with my wife and kids being threatened?"

"Sounds like it's a miscommunication that never was able to be worked out when you left town," I said, looking at Mr. Tobias. "Mr. Richardson was the mayor here?"

"Jolie, I know you mean well, deary. There's a lot to this. Yes, Rex and Roxi's dad was a mayor for one term only."

"That doesn't surprise me," I mumbled under my breath—taking note. Also, Mr. Tobias seemed to be skirting around an issue. He looked innocent enough and I'm sure I felt that way even more because he was a dear friend's dad I'd known growing up. Ava warned me in our PI lessons not to allow emotions to weigh in on investigations, but it was difficult for me.

"There really is a lot to this. I'm not sure it's anything that can be fixed over a cup of weak decaf coffee," Tom said, getting up and slamming down a few bills and stomping out.

"Hey," I said to no one as Harvey grinned at me, gave me a bump on my shoulder and took off. There was no need to stoop to insults on my coffee. I took a sniff then dipped a clean spoon into the half-filled cup and tasted. "Blech! Who made this coffee?" I yelled back at my family.

I opened the door and dropped my tote on the chair and fell to the couch.

"Long day?" Mick asked, walking out from the hallway. He lifted my legs, pulled my tennis shoes off, and began rubbing my feet.

I moaned inwardly. "Yes. Mary is awake now. Delilah took Mirabelle to see her. Ava's moods are all over the place. Family. Older men acting like children." I summed up my day monotonously lifting an arm over my head for flare. "I'm exhausted."

"I feel like you and I have been passing ships in the night the last several days." He took his thumb and pushed it into the arch of my foot, knowing it helped ease some sciatic pain. I groaned.

"There's a lot we need to talk about," Mick said, nudging my legs.

I drug my limp body into a sitting position. "I know."

"First off, what happened with my mother and my sister when you went out with them?"

What did happen with them? So much had

transpired within the last week. "A lot of miscommunication. Plus, I was overly emotional. I think I still felt sick. It comes and goes. It really wasn't that big of a deal. You know how I get sometimes."

"Okay," he said skeptically. "You know you do not ever have to try and get their approval. Ever."

"I know. Your turn. Who is Imelda to you really?" I brought my chin to my chest, narrowing my eyes at him.

"I knew this was coming," Mick groaned, then rolled his brown eyes. "A kid crush is all—oy—she's like a Wonder Woman Amazon woman—you saw her." Mick said, holding his right hand about two feet over his head signalling her height.

Mick was a tall man, but she did tower over him. "Boy, I just LOVE to hear that you have Wonder Woman chasing after you!"

Mick moved closer and put his arms around me. "Are you jealous?" He nuzzled my neck with his lips. He knew that drove me nuts.

"Yes, I am. I used to have Wonder Woman underroos."

Mick continued to nibble on my neck then my ear and whispered, "Want to be my Wonder Woman tonight?"

Um, duh!

Chapter Eleven

It was Saturday afternoon, before the prom, and the crew was meeting at our house. We had finally finished unpacking everything. Okay, not everything. There was still a large army green burlap bag filled with shoes sitting in the corner of our bedroom, but the guests wouldn't see that. I had made iced tea and some cast iron snacks for our meeting in a few minutes and to take to the prom tonight as finger foods. I stood at the counter of our kitchen arranging the fried ravioli with marinara sauce, fried beef flautas, and fried dill pickles on a tray. I put the deep-fried Oreo cookies off to the side of the counter to have with coffee and hot tea later if there was time.

"I know you all want to talk about the case, Jolie," Mick said walking into the living room. "But you know there is only so much I can share."

Okay—I see he hadn't gotten over our earlier conversation about being open-minded about what we would discuss at today's meeting. "I know, but there are some things you need to be here for. Trust me," I said, laying the tray of snacks on the coffee table. I didn't fill him in on anything Tabitha had told us in confidence but he was nervous to be associated with the case outside of "official" channels.

Mick bent over for a ravioli and dunked it in the sauce, popping it in his mouth. Immediately, his eyes bulged out.

"Good, right?" I said.

He shook his head, mimicking a breeze with his hand, signaling it was still very hot.

"Oh yeah, I just pulled them out of the Dutch pot so they could cool down for the guests." I winced. "Sorry!"

I noticed a tiny tear well up from the scalding grease that was probably burning his tongue now.

"Ehth ohay," he said without moving his tongue. He snatched up his glass and chugged some iced tea.

The door jiggled and Mick gave me an odd look as a key opened it.

"It's Ava." I shrugged.

"You gave her a key?" he asked more normally.

"No," I said as she and Delilah came inside.

"I told you we should have knocked," Delilah scolded, looking from me to Mick, then covering her face with her hands in embarrassment.

"It's okay, we've already had that argument." I waved off her concerns and ignored Mick's stern look.

"Tabitha isn't here?" Ava asked, going for the ravioli.

"Don't!" Mick yelled, reaching out.

"Dude, you put the snacks on the table for us to eat, yes?" Ava growled and popped one in her mouth, chewing slowly and moaning her satisfaction.

"That didn't burn your mouth?"

"Nah, I'm used to it by now. These are delish!" She picked up a mug for tea.

"Tabitha's not here yet, but I think I just heard a car door." I said as I crossed past Laurel and Hardy to the door and opened it so she could come inside.

"Hey guys," Tabitha said, then cleared her throat as she studied Mick's face. She was using her profiling to see if we'd told him anything yet. She seemed satisfied and sat down.

"Want some tea?" I asked, not knowing where to start and suddenly dreading the upcoming conversation. Instead, I took six deep-fried dill pickles and shoved three into my mouth at once.

"I'm fine for now." Tabitha took a shaky breath. "Mick, I told them."

I gulped a huge greasy sour slimy treat loudly and choked on it. I held my arm up to assure everyone I was fine.

Mick scratched his chin as his eyebrows squished together. "You told them how much?"

"They know why I'm here. Well, kind of. They know that I initially came here undercover and that it changed into an actual therapy position. They know why I helped them push through the PI license. They know about me and Teddy—again, kind of."

Mick sat silent, letting it all sink in.

"And I figured out what the tunnels were used for in the twenties," I said, seeing Ava's head jerk toward me.

"You never told *me*!"

"I was trying to keep you out of things," I said, looking to Delilah.

Ava glared at her wife.

"Prohibition, and I'm assuming drugs, and who knows what else," I finished.

Mick eyed me. I couldn't tell if he was upset and worried I'd been digging around or if he was wondering if I was ready to murder him for not telling me this. Even though, rationally, I KNEW we both had agreed some things couldn't be shared, the irrational me was ready to beat him senseless.

"Also, I think we should share that we have come to realize there is a mole in Leavensport. I have no clue who it is yet, but someone here is tied to all of this," I said, noticing that Ava was staring daggers at me. "What? They are obviously doing all this undercover stuff here because of the connection."

Ava's eyebrows rose toward Mick. "Is that why you came here to begin with?"

I swung my head toward him.

"Y- - -es," Mick said slowly, shrugging his shoulders. He took one look at my hurt expression and said quickly, "I never lied to you. I was here helping Teddy. I told you there's been some undercover work."

I nodded my head slowly, not moving my eyes. "We need to keep to the agenda if we are going to make it on time to help Missy. So, yes, everyone new to Leavensport is somehow undercover. Let's check that off the list," I said, tongue-in-cheek, feeling myself fume internally. I was so furious right now I was ready to blow! "Someone should tell me what's going on with Carlos."

"Jolie—" Mick started.

"I. Don't. Care. Do NOT tell me you can't share it!"

"Carlos was the other man on the video at Janelle's murder," Tabitha said.

"How could you know that?" Mick asked incredulously.

"He didn't do it. She was my cousin, Mick, and I'm telling you he didn't do that." Tabitha looked hard at Mick.

"I know he didn't do it. It doesn't mean I don't have to do my job. Teddy told you it was a conflict of interest for you to be on this case," he warned.

Wow, no one seemed too happy with each other this afternoon.

I changed the subject, hoping that would lessen the tension in the air. "I heard Mary and Jorge are both going to be fine."

"True, but Mary's got to be sick over Carlos. Also, you guys released Darrell and do you know no one has seen him since?" Tabitha said. She was having none of my attempts to ease tension.

"Again, how do you know all of this?" Mick gritted his teeth.

"Seems your wife understands the best business to be in to actually get to the truth. I just followed suit." Tabitha leaned back and crossed her arms and legs simultaneously on the couch.

"Okay, let's just all take a breath—" I started.

"Nope, I'm not going to sit here and get fried by four women." Mick took long strides to his safe for his shield and gun and started toward the door.

"You forgot irrational," I fired back. "Four. *Irrational!* WOMEN!"

He paused in the doorframe. I watched his

back expand as he inhaled, then collapse as he exhaled. Then his head snapped around. He turned around to face his firing squad.

"I'm sorry." He took a long pause, pondering a thought. "I'm sorry I'm trying to do my job. Trying to follow the rules. Trying to stay on the legal side of things. Worrying about my wife. Yes, I know you are more than just my wife. But you are also my wife and I love you! And I'm sorry I care about all of you women and worry about you all getting hurt physically or emotionally in this twisted web."

He left, slamming the door behind him for emphasis.

The four of us sat in silence for a moment before Ava broke the stillness.

"What a baby!" she exclaimed.

Delilah, Tabitha, and I all looked at each other with wrinkled foreheads for a moment awkwardly. Next, BOOMS of laughter exploded from all four of us.

I slapped my leg while squealing, "Poor guy! He was so serious and so nice. We are all horrible!" I grabbed another handful of the deep-fried dill pickles and wolfed them down.

"Aw, he probably knows we're laughing at him right now," Ava giggled. "He obviously knows you, Jolie, meaning he knows what you and your friends are like." She shrugged.

She was right. On cue, my phone buzzed, and I looked down. Mick was Face-Timing me.

I didn't answer immediately, but held it down like it was a secret and whispered while giggling, "It's him. He's Face-Timing me. You guys, shush!"

I pressed the button, doing my best to put on a shameful face. "Hi, honey," I said.

He stared hard at me for a full moment.

I smiled sweetly, then we both cracked up and I held the phone up around the women who all joined in a hearty laugh.

"Sorry," Tabitha cleared her throat. "I haven't been myself lately."

"I know, and I'm going to pretend I heard none of what was said and I don't want to know what you all discuss after I hang up." He looked at me knowingly.

He was so much of a better person than I could ever be.

"So how do you know all that?" I asked Tabitha when Mick disconnected.

"Janelle's girlfriend worked with her on this case," Tabitha said. "No one knew they were a couple or they'd never be allowed to work together. She's feeding me information."

"How'd you find out about Darrell?" I asked next. "Janelle's girlfriend wouldn't know that."

"You're getting good at the observation part of PI work," Tabitha grinned and shook her index finger at me. "Keith told me."

Ava's, Delilah's, and my head did not move, but our eyeballs circled around, looking around at each of us.

"Why would Keith tell you that?" I asked.

"Again, you are getting good at knowing what questions to ask too," Tabitha praised. "Are you reading Ava's PI textbooks?"

"I have read some of them recently." I smiled at the praise.

"Diverting the conversation," Ava scolded me. "You just let her use your emotions to divert answering your question."

I glowered at Tabitha.

"So, answer the lady," Ava said.

"Keith and I are seeing each other." Tabitha looked down at the floor.

"Wait, WHAT?" This was the somewhat close reaction from all of us, minus a few expletives from Ava—I'm assuming it's those baby hormones.

"I knew you weren't seeing Teddy, but I thought Keith was seeing Marissa?" I asked. I felt like I had to take my hand and push my jaw up from where it had landed on the floor from shock.

"He's not," Tabitha said, putting her tongue in her cheek so it bulged a little.

That was a typical response to someone covering something up, so I told Tabitha that and I wasn't going to mind more praise.

This time Tabitha didn't seem to feel pride. "More stuff you can't know."

"Got it," I created the thumb-finger gun and shot invisible bullets her way, then reached for the laptop to add a note to the I Spy slides. I hated how satisfied I felt adding this information.

"Wait, what did I just miss?" Ava asked, looking from me to Tabitha and back to me again.

"Jolie just realized that Keith is pretending to date Marissa because the FBI thinks she's connected somehow," Delilah explained, showing Ava both of her palms as they faced the ceiling with an *Elementary My Dear Watson* tone of voice.

I grinned at Delilah and saw Tabitha flash a smile at Ava like the cat that just ate the canary.

"I've been sick lately, so—I'm just off my game right now." Ava pouted.

"So, why did they let Darrell go?" I asked Tabitha.

"They found out he had an alibi. A woman who was living on the street that had recently gotten to the shelter said he was with her and Devonte vowed that he saw them together at the time of the murder." Tabitha reached up for tea and selected a plate of snacks, which were cold by now.

She took a drink and continued. "Carlos doesn't have an alibi. He was there because he got a call from the people who offered him the loan. They told him to be at the homeless shelter at exactly seven p.m. They set him up."

"But can the police make a solid connection other than him being there at the right time?" Ava asked.

"No," Tabitha said, "but they can hold him for seventy-two hours, and that's what they're doing while trying to find something that can connect him to it."

"But none of them believe Carlos did this. You don't think he did it and you matter the most. Why are they wasting their time looking into someone they know did not do this?" I bellowed. "I mean, I get it. Do your job, but hold him for seventy-two hours and let him go!"

"I'm not the most important person here, Jolie," Tabitha started. "The FBI lost one of their own. They will not take that lightly and they will catch the person who did this and make them pay."

I felt my stomach begin to lurch as I feared for Carlos's future. I jumped up and ran to the bathroom and threw up.

Several minutes had passed and I was sure I'd gotten all of the snacks out of my system. I looked at my phone and realized we needed to start getting ready to head out to chaperone.

"You okay?" Delilah asked.

"Yeah, I have that stomach flu but it's really hit or miss." I rubbed my stomach.

"You canceling tonight?" Ava asked.

"No way, I'm fine now that I got sick."

"Okay, well girls, I'm going to take off. I'll be at my office most of tonight," Tabitha said, getting up from the couch and stretching left to right from her waist. "Actually, I might sleep on the couch. I need to spend some time adding to my notes and going over everything."

"So, do weekends count?" I asked Tabitha as she was heading out the door.

"Huh?" Tabitha and Ava asked simultaneously.

"The seventy-two hours for Carlos."

"Oh, holidays and weekends aren't included. He'll get out Tuesday afternoon if they can't find evidence to connect him," Tabitha said, and waved as she shut the door.

"We need to get ready," Ava said frantically.

"You sure you don't want me to take Mirabelle tonight?" Delilah asked.

"No," I said, "the women in my family are more than thrilled they get to spoil her for the evening."

"I might go check on her before and after the prom if I have time," Ava said, reaching for a garment bag.

Huh, she must have pressed pants for tonight. That's nice.

"She's going to make a fantastic mom. I have to be honest, I didn't know when I first heard. Not you, Delilah." I held up a hand to not to insult her.

"This one."

Ava shoved me hard.

"What?" I laughed, pushing her back. "No seriously, though, the last week I've watched you protect Luis at the shelter, then you jumped into action with Mirabelle. Like saying you want to check in on her before and after prom." I rocked my arms back and forth in a motherly way.

"You really have been better with Mirabelle than me," Delilah said.

"Not to mention Mirabelle seems to favor you and just ADORE you." I held the vowel out for extra emphasis, grinning, then hip-bumped her. Ava had always been more on the self-involved side. She was showing another side of herself or discovering it for the first time.

Delilah was grinning ear to ear at her wife carrying their child in her belly, and my heart swelled.

It was half past six and I arrived late, with just enough time to help set up. Ava was taking way too long in the bathroom, so I yelled through the door that I was going over and she'd have to drive herself. I'd darted out when the expletives started from the door again. I couldn't wait to tell my little niece or nephew how horrible their mama was while pregnant with them.

"Jolie, you made it." Missy came scurrying over to me in her tan slacks and pastel floral blouse.

"Yeah, Ava's right behind me. Sorry, I couldn't get her out of the bathroom."

"She isn't still sick, is she?" Missy asked.

"Oh-uh, no. She hasn't been out in a while so I

think she was playing with her hair."

"Okay, well, if you can help blow up some more balloons and put those strings on them and make a grouping of each color for each side of the photo booth, that would be great!"

"Wait, photo booth? Isn't there going to be a photographer? You know, dance pictures where you pay for a package?"

Missy giggled at me. "Um, yeah, maybe a decade ago. The kids use their funds for photo booths and for props for selfie-stations." She pointed at an area with a photo booth and outside of it were three different prop settings with loads of fun costume stuff I wanted to play with.

I looked around for the first time and realized it was a masquerade ball theme, which I thought was pretty cool. Two of the settings for the selfie-station were the masque ball from *Romeo and Juliet* and the other was *A Midsummer Night's Dream*-themed. I'm sure that those were the high school English teachers' choices. The third setting looked like a Harlequin romance novel that was pushing the boundaries on erotica. I'm sure that was not a teacher's idea, but some teen group seeing how close to the line they could get.

I smiled at Missy, who was looking at the door that had just slammed open. Ava came strutting in with a light brown sleeveless dress that had a large burgundy bow tie at the breast. The dress lay nicely, tightening at her waist and then flaring out. The issue was the sock puppet monkeys that were sewn over the entire skirt.

Missy's mouth fell open, then she quickly shut it. "Ava, thank you so much for doing this for the kids."

I looked at Missy like she was insane. Why was she acting like this wasn't the most ridiculous thing she'd ever seen?

"What are you wearing?" I asked, looking at my gray Gitano stretch jeans with a light-threaded short-sleeved burgundy sweater and my Birk clogs.

"What? Kids will love these!" Ava looked down at her skirt and grinned.

Missy leaned in to whisper to me. "She's been acting so crazy lately, I wouldn't be surprised if she was expecting!" She giggled, shaking her head, and walked off.

"Okay, we have a job to do. Let's go, Sweat Socks. Wait, is that material like sweat socks?" I asked, reaching in to feel the fabric and purposely *not* telling Ava what Missy just said.

Ava laughed. "It is! That makes it even better!"

I had a feeling Ava and I may be laughed out of the prom at some point tonight.

Later that night, the kids showed up all decked out. I was surprised to find that half the students wore traditional long, sequined dresses with plunging necklines and tuxes for the guys. The other half had silly costumes. One girl had a dress that was blue on one side and red on the other. The blue side had a huge picture of Jacob from *Twilight* and the red side had Edward. Bella's face was in the center, over the girl's heart. I saw a strapless green Mountain Dew-canned girl with a green-sequin-suited boy.

"Nice," green Mountain Dew dude said to Ava, checking out her dress.

"You too, my man," Ava said, pointing at his suit.

"See, you are the one who looks like a teacher!"

Ava spouted at me after her main fizz took off.

"Yeah, I'm good with that," I said, sipping some punch. Missy had moved us from balloon duty to punch duty and Ava was taking her job very seriously.

"I'll need you to hand over the jacket," Ava said to a stocky, muscular jock.

"Excuse me, ma'am?" The jock asked politely, flashing his pearly smile at her.

"It won't work on me. You can try your desperate smile on Barbie over here," Ava jerked her head toward me. "Now, give me the jacket before you get your punch AND pull your pockets out."

"Ava!" I said reproachfully.

The football-player-looking teen grinned my way, shrugging his shoulders.

"No, it won't work on me either," I said, pointing at the jacket.

He skulked off, mumbling something under his breath at us.

Ava jerked her head up and brought her walkie talkie up to her mouth. "Incoming. Your three o'clock." She unclicked the button and listened, then continued. "Yeah, the one with the Justin Bieber look."

"Got him," said a voice through the speaker.

"What is that?"

"A walkie talkie," Ava gave me the *duh* stare.

"Who are you talking to?"

"Mr. Santiago! You remember him, right?"

A girl with a clasped purse came up to get some punch.

"What do you need that purse for?" Ava asked, stepping in front of the pretty blonde with long waves of hair flowing down her back. She looked like a princess in her pastel pink and blue taffeta covered dress.

"Um, I keep my phone and my lipstick in it." The girl looked terrified.

I didn't think she was trying to get away with anything. "You're fine, go ahead."

The girl looked at me, then hesitantly at Ava, and took a timid step, reaching for a plastic cup.

"I've got my eye on you, missy!" Ava said.

The Disney princess looked at Ava's dress, eyes wide like Bambi, and smiled, got a ladle of punch, and rushed away as fast as possible.

"Is that who you are talking to?" I asked. "Mr. Santiago?"

Ava laughed. "Yep, do you remember when Riley Snarl spiked the punch and we didn't know he did it?"

"How could I forget? You drank too much and puked red punch up all over my off-white dress."

Ava cracked up as a line formed for the punch.

"The problem was, that isn't the only time you've puked on me," I said, signaling for the next student to step up so we could search them for contraband.

A bit more time passed and the line for punch had died down and it looked like the bathroom was the next of the long lines. I was starting to get bored and looked at my watch. I rubbed my stomach and looked at the line to the bathroom.

"You aren't getting sick again, are you?" Ava asked, eyeing my hand rubbing my stomach.

"Every time I think I'm over it, it comes back."

"Maybe you're pregnant too," Ava said.

"I beg your pardon?"

Ava's brown eyes lit up. "Oh my gosh, that would be A—MAZING!"

"I'm not pregnant, Ava. We weren't trying and I'm on the pill. We're overly cautious. I've got whatever has been going around."

I saw a scuffle on the dance floor out of the corner of my eye. It looked like a few guys were gathered around someone.

Ava and I looked around and didn't see any adults so we walked over to check it out.

Luis Sanchez was standing with a young man who was a bit shorter than Luis. Both boys wore tuxes and the boy with Luis had a pink cummerbund on. The three other boys were making fun of him.

"Back off, man." Luis shoved a stocky kid who towered over the boy with the pink cummerbund.

"Luis, let it go," I said, reaching for him.

"These jerks are giving me and Jarrod a hard time because they aren't comfortable in their masculinity," Luis spat out toward the group.

I noticed Ava's body tighten and I squeezed my eyes shut. She had a tendency to overreact at closed-minded people. I tried to tell her before everyone had a right to their beliefs and feelings as long as no one was hurting anyone—but hurting went beyond the physical and that included bullying to make people feel less than like this group of boys were doing to Luis and his date.

"Hey guys, listen, I'm standing here in a sock monkey dress on a Saturday night to help you all be able to enjoy your prom. So yeah, these guys are dancing and maybe they are dating and this guy has pink on—I mean, seriously, are you so bored that you have to be mean? Or are you insecure or are people mean to you? I mean, why are you acting like this?"

I was completely shocked at how calm, unthreatening, and matter-of-fact my friend was being right now.

"They're just—" Luis started in anger.

Ava turned toward him. "Luis, if you are bi or gay, you are going to need to get rid of that anger. You are going to find a world full of people who don't understand you and that is okay. They have a right to their beliefs. They don't have a right to make you feel less than, though. Educating people and then giving them space to make their own decisions and supporting them even if you don't agree with them is the best thing you can do. Then, you get to be happy and hope the same for them."

I felt tears well up in my eyes. Ava sounded so grown up. I mean, I knew we were grown up now—had been for a while, but I was realizing how much of our early twenties was about figuring out who we were as women and we were finally feeling it.

"Hey man, sorry, no hard feelings," said the student who had been menacing them. "Sock-monkey is right. I was bored and being dumb." He looked at his buddies and pulled their sleeves away.

"Wow, you did it," I told Ava.

Ava had a look of pride.

I turned around and saw Mr. Santiago, all six-foot-four of him, towering over us, glaring toward the boys who had just run off. My old teacher grinned at me, putting a finger to his lips signaling me not to tell and moved into the dance crowd before Ava could see him.

Only one more hour and I could go home, pet some kitty heads, take a shower, get a cup of tea, read or watch TV until my hubby got home. One thing I'd learned about myself is that I was still a homebody and a kitchen was my favorite place to be.

Speaking of, I looked down and saw the cast iron snacks were running low. I went back to the kitchen area to reheat enough food to last one more hour. I figured if these got eaten I wouldn't replace them with any more, so I packed up the rest of the snacks and started cleaning up the kitchen.

"I think you're beautiful," I heard a man say.

I froze and wondered if I should make myself known. I mean, if it was a teen and his date then they shouldn't be making out back here. I listened for another moment.

"Bobby, thank you. This is our first date, so let's keep it casual."

That was Betsy. Awkward. I stood very still, afraid if I tried to leave they'd hear me.

"Come on," I heard Bobby say.

I started to move, but heard a grunt and saw Betsy storm back out to the prom.

Bobby came limping behind, then shook it off and moved out the door.

I knew I didn't like that guy. I needed to start trusting my instincts more.

I hurried out of the kitchen walking toward my friend. Just as I reached her, a tall person shoved me and I stumbled into Ava, forcing her to splash the big cup of red punch she was holding all over my gray jeans. "Oh man! Great!" I yelled out.

Several students stopped, looked, and laughed. Nice.

"Who was that?" I said, looking and seeing a tall, dark-haired woman moving quickly through the dance floor. *Imelda?*

Ava had run back to the kitchen for some baking soda and an apron and came back, making a paste to soak up the stain and putting an apron around me. "There. Now, what happened?"

"I think that was Imelda." I pointed in the direction that she had disappeared.

"Huh, why would she be here?"

Right? Why?

"Jolie, what were you going to say before I plastered you yet again with red punch?"

"Oh, I called Tabitha," I said. "She's staying at the office tonight like she thought. Let's go talk to her after we're done here. I feel like she'll tell us more after the meeting we had this afternoon. Plus, I think it's time we showed her some of our cards, too."

"Seriously, what is this music the kids listen to today?" Ava moaned. "It's like a hammer pounding in my head."

"I don't know. I think I heard Cyclone, some Tipsy too," I said.

"You're not that hip." Ava took a step back in surprise.

"Okay, I overheard some girls talking about the music. How would I know this stuff?"

I marched up to the D.J. and recommended a song that Ava and I used to sing and dance to multiple times a day.

The next song that came on was Beyonce's

"Single Ladies" and Ava and I looked at each other excitedly and started mouthing all the words and doing the little dance we came up with for it. Two steps left, two steps right, hop to the front, move two steps back, clap, clap, right leg shake. Pretty soon, a few of the other oddly dressed teens started following us, and before long, most of the teens, except for the super cool ones, took to the floor, doing our moves. It was a moment to remember for sure!

The music changed back to modern day nonsense and I noticed Bobby beeline for the door, and then I saw Asher and Caleb again. I moved through the dance floor, working to keep my eye on them between bobbing heads. I got through the crowd in time to see Bobby hand a bag of something to Asher. Asher opened the bag and pulled out what looked to be a bundle of money; although, I couldn't be sure.

Asher looked up and caught my eye before I could look away. He stood staring for a long moment and I held his gaze. His gaze went to a glare, then a vile smirk.

Betsy came up behind me. "Hey, Jolie, Ava is looking for—"

I pointed to where Bobby was and we both looked. Asher and Caleb grabbed him and he struggled for a moment before they dragged him out the door.

We ran to the door, but by the time we got outside, there was a white van heading out of the parking lot. The van had a busted taillight on the right side—just like Nestle's van the night of the Janelle's murder.

Chapter Twelve

Betsy called the police and Mr. Santiago sent all the chaperones other than Betsy outside to keep an eye on the kids who were waiting for their rides and to make sure those that drove got to their cars safely. He sent several group texts to the parents of the kids at the prom, letting them know what happened. This would have been a job for Bobby Zane, except he seemed to be somehow involved in the criminal activity. Unfortunately, it appeared to have turned on him.

I saw a squad car pull up and Teddy got out, moving quickly toward me. "Where's Betsy? Is she okay?"

"She's fine. She's waiting in the kitchen," I said, pointing inside.

"You were with her when the guy was taken?" Teddy asked.

I nodded.

He motioned with a finger for me to follow him. I looked to Mr. Santiago, who saw the exchange and nodded in understanding.

Betsy stood up and smoothed her green skirt

down when she saw Teddy.

"Hey, you okay?" Teddy rubbed her arm.

"Yeah, I was—I was—um," Betsy looked at me helplessly.

"She was on a date with Bobby tonight," I explained. "We can't tell you much, we saw him talking to Asher and Caleb from the construction company Nestle runs. I saw Bobby hand them something in a small bag. I thought it was a bundle of money but I was kind of far away so I can't be sure."

"Wait, back up. You're positive it was Caleb and Asher, though, right?" Teddy had his pad out, writing it all down.

"Yeah, Ava and I saw the three of them talking in the parking lot late one night and they were in the same white van." I recalled the night Ava told me she was pregnant and my sudden stop at the school.

"When was this?" Teddy asked.

"A week or a little more ago, I think."

"How do you know it was the same van?" Teddy asked.

"Because it was the same van Nestle had at the murder scene," I said.

Betsy looked from me to Teddy.

Teddy looked at me expectantly.

"Remember? I told you that you could cite him for the right taillight being busted. Same thing. We ran outside but saw the van speeding off and it was dark out again. I noticed the taillight."

"Okay, I got what I need for now. Betsy, can I drive you home?" Teddy asked.

I was happy he was taking her home. Maybe

those two would have a chance to catch up.

Ava popped up behind me. "Tabitha just texted asking if we are stopping by the office."

"Yes, you go ahead since you drove separately. I'm going to get the dishes and run them to the restaurant real quick and I'll be right behind you," I said, heading back to the kitchen for the three warming bags filled with dirty Tupperware and trays from our restaurant.

I parked in the alley and went to unlock the door and turn the alarm off before getting the warmers. I was just going to load the dishwasher and soak any dishes that needed it overnight, then head to Tabitha's office.

I got out of my car and turned my phone flashlight on to help me see my keys and moved to the door. Without thinking, I flashed the light around the alley. I hadn't heard anything but too many crazy things had happened in the last three years and I got nervous being alone in an alley at night. I never would have felt this way five years ago. So much had changed in our little town—yet, it seemed like the more I found out the longer a dark cloud had hung over this place and I had been clueless.

I turned the alarm off, hefted the bags, ran into the shop, locked the door and took a deep sigh of relief. Okay, I started gathering the dirty dishes and sorting them for the dishwasher and what needed to be soaked.

My phone buzzed and I figured it had to be Ava. "I'm on my way. I'll be there in less than five minutes."

"It's not your sidekick," a strangled voice said.

"Who is this? Asher? Caleb? We saw you."

"You've always been nosey. All the way back when your poor old grandma was a suspect in beloved Ellie Siler's death."

Was that a female voice? I couldn't tell. The sound kept going from a high-pitched squeal to a lower registered baritone voice sounding like a man. I pulled my phone away from my ear and could hear something from the office off to the side of the kitchen. I looked at the door out to the alley where my car sat just beyond it and then looked at the office door I'd have to pass to get there.

I looked around the kitchen, moving to the closed office door slowly, with my heart pounding so hard I could feel the beating in my eardrums. I paused momentarily to listen and could hear a noise similar to what was coming from my phone. I hung up and pushed the office door open slowly, feeling every muscle in my body tighten.

The sound cut off and I flipped the light on. No one was there. There was a tape-recording device I didn't recognize on the desk with a note taped to it. It was a picture of me and Ava together at the prom with a huge red X across both of our faces.

Ten minutes later, Tabitha and Ava arrived to pick me up. I'd called to tell them what had happened and where I was. Tabitha had told me not to touch anything. She'd arrived with gloves and a special greenish light to look at the doors and the recorder and the paper.

"Whoever did this wore gloves and wiped things down, but maybe we can do some digging on this old device and come up with something." Tabitha flipped the light on and held the device up. "Yeah, this is an old machine."

"You two okay to stay here? I can heat up some leftovers and we have plenty to drink."

"Fine with me," Tabitha said.

"Has anyone heard from Darrell?" I asked.

"Right now, Darrell, Bobby, and Lia seem to be missing," Tabitha said.

Ava and I looked at each other. That wasn't a card I was willing to show Tabitha yet.

"Lia?" I faked surprise.

"Yeah, I went to the shelter to talk to her and Devonte, but he said he hadn't seen her for a few days. I didn't ask where she was, so I suppose she could be out of town, but it still seems odd. She wasn't there the night Janelle was murdered, either."

"So, when the person called, they knew what I said. They knew I thought I was talking to Ava, after that is when it sounded like a recording and when I heard things in the office," I said to Tabitha.

"Yeah, it's an old device where they hook their number to this machine. Once they make the call and say something, it signals for the recorded message to take over. I'm guessing you guys are being watched and someone knew you'd stop by here tonight?"

"I think whoever did this isn't necessarily involved in your cousin's murder. Maybe. But the recording mentioned Ellie Siler. I think the Leavensport mole contacted me," I said, reaching for the tape after Tabitha was done checking it.

"That was something we wanted to share with you tonight," Ava said.

"What's that?" Tabitha asked.

"Do you know who is behind things here in town?" I asked Tabitha.

"I don't, and I'd tell you if it was something I

couldn't share with you. I truly don't. We've been speculating though."

"So have we," Ava said.

"I mean, Harvey shows back up and things get weird. Tom Costello's got a murky past and can't seem to give concrete answers on anything," I said.

"Maybe it's both of them," Tabitha said.

"But they both came in here the other night, arguing in front of me and my family," I said.

"Maybe they wanted you to see that," Tabitha said.

"This is getting to be like a spy novel," Ava said, snatching up a deep-fried Oreo, eating it in one bite, and moaning. "Uh—so good!"

Tabitha and I took one too. I wasn't much of a coffee drinker but it had been a really long day and I needed something to perk me up fast, so I made us a pot.

"We should have gone back to my office. I have my laptop there," Tabitha said.

"No worries," Ava said, looking at me.

I zipped open my tote bag and pulled out my Microsoft Surface.

Tabitha grinned.

"She's like a party trick. Ask for anything and Jolie will pull it out of her purse." Ava did an abracadabra move.

"You know, the only time I've smiled or laughed since Janelle was killed is with the two of you," Tabitha said.

We both gave her a hug and she let us for a moment, then shooed us away.

"Janelle always looked up to me," Tabitha said. "I wish she could have just joined the FBI and not gotten caught up in this case."

I bit my tongue, wanting to remind her of playing the what-if or should-have/could-have games. She'd had to tell me that often in our sessions. It was one thing to say it and a whole other thing to put it into practice when you were beating yourself up.

"Okay," I said, pulling up a new fresh slide. "Throw suspects out at me—go through all the questions starting with who."

"Asher, Caleb, and Nestle and why is it that van seems to connect them all," Ava said.

I nodded, typing. "You're right. We've seen Asher and Caleb use it with Bobby at the school. It's the same van Nestle was driving at the murder scene."

"Harvey and Tom since they are acting weird," Tabitha said.

"But I'm making a note that they may be part of the bigger picture," I said while typing.

"You know you want to list Imelda," Ava teased me.

"I would love to add her," I started. "I'd love to get her arrested for something—but I heard Mick's sister talking to her on the phone after Janelle's murder. Imelda was in Italy then." I rolled my eyes.

"Trouble in paradise?" Tabitha asked.

"Nah, just a childhood crush," I said. "Although, I guess I don't know who was crushing on whom."

Ava yawned loudly.

"Yeah, it's late, ladies." Tabitha looked at her watch.

I looked at the time on my laptop. It was close

to midnight. Mick hadn't called me yet, so I assumed he was caught up in something with the case. I hoped it was something that cleared Carlos' name.

We all went to the alley together. Tabitha took the recording device with the picture of Ava and I with her. She wanted to look into it more.

I couldn't help but feel we were getting closer to something. What—well, I wasn't sure of that—yet.

When I got home, I saw that Delilah had texted, telling me Ava had checked on Mirabelle after she left the restaurant. Delilah had told Ava to sleep in this morning and that I should do the same thing. She was picking Mirabelle up from my mom's house and mom and Aunt Fern would open the restaurant for us in the morning. I was not arguing.

I did exactly that. Slept in and woke up to a note that Mick had gotten home about an hour after me, but I was out of it. It was eight thirty and he had already left to meet Keith for a round of golf.

Mick and I had done a lot of research about the best types of sports and exercising for those with MS. The key was to do it in moderation, not pushing too hard. Mick struggled with that when it came to work and that often is what caused setbacks for him. A relaxing game of golf would do him good.

I got up and got dressed, then texted my mom.

Morning, thanks for opening for us.

No prob, everything is fine here. Take ur time.

I gave her a thumbs up emoji and made some hot tea and a bowl of Cheerios, then reached for my journal.

I figured I'd have a little breakfast and get some thoughts out before going in to work.

I think the biggest thing bothering me right now is that Mick and I are married and living together but we haven't had any time in the last couple of weeks to sit and talk. And we really need to. Ugh, I feel like this is always going to be an issue as long as he's with the police force and Ava and I are pursuing this ongoing case with the history of this town.

I still can't believe how lucky I am to have found my soulmate. If I was writing this entry eight months ago, I'd be terrified the relationship would be over. It still boggles my mind how so much can change so quickly but how I still feel the same in many ways.

I took a few bites of my Cheerios and slurped some tea, thinking about how many trust issues I had with men for most of my life.

I still doubted I'd ever trust my biological father again, but with Mick, it's nice to be able to believe in someone again.

I went back into freewriting, momentarily lost in thought.

Trust. Fathers. Teddy's father. He left his wife and kid. Tom Costello stayed and said he did what he did to save his family. What about Karl Davis or Lory Davis for that matter? Darrell was a dad. Now Carlos is a dad . . .

Yikes, I didn't realize I'd spent so much time thinking. I needed to get to work.

A few hours later, I was busy cleaning up from the

lunch rush and prepping for the dinner crowd when Mick came into the kitchen.

"Hey, stranger," I said, giving a cute finger wave with my soapy hands as he reached for a hug. "You okay?"

I stepped back and picked up a towel to dry off.

"Yeah, I've just missed my wife. I'm sorry I left before you woke up this morning. I needed some fresh air and to get my mind off of things."

"I get it, babe. Seriously, I was writing in my journal how I would have been terrified several months ago about our relationship if this stuff was going on. I don't feel that way at all now. I know we'll be fine no matter what." I rubbed his hands.

"Do you two need to go get a room together?" Ava asked, strolling into the office.

"I think we do," Mick said.

"Gross," Ava said, grabbing something and running back up front.

I giggled. "You actually taking a full day off today?"

"I just got back from seeing Tabitha," he said.

"Oh, how is she doing?" I asked, feeling odd that I'd just seen her last night. Mick didn't know that or about the phone call. But he knew about Asher, Caleb, and Bobby from Teddy.

"I don't know. She seemed—off. But I can't put my finger on it. Anyway, I'm here to see if you are coming home with me tonight?"

My cell buzzed in a text message. I checked it, seeing it was from Tabitha.

I found something after you left last night. I need you to meet me at the park past the gazebo at the green iron bench.

I texted back, *Now?!?* Then I looked up at Mick, smiling.

Bzzz. I looked down at my phone. *Now. I know where Darrell is and you need to know too.*

"So I take it we don't get an evening together," Mick said.

"I'm sorry," I said, hugging him.

"You aren't doing anything dangerous, are you?" he asked.

"No, Tabitha just texted and wants me to meet her for a minute," I said. "Maybe she'll tell me what's up with her. Although, she's been through a lot. She is grieving, you know."

"You're right, I can't imagine what she's feeling," Mick said. "Can you drop this file off at the station with Teddy on your way, please?"

"Sure thing," I said, reaching up to kiss him as Bea Seevers came in to relieve me for the evening. She, Magda, and Ava were going to close tonight.

Chapter Thirteen

I drove to the police station before going to meet Tabitha. The sun was beginning to set and I got to witness another beautiful dusk in Leavensport. I loved the seasons here in Ohio and Leavensport had always been such a beautiful town. I'd not been enjoying the scenery as much lately with so much turmoil.

I jammed on my breaks as some moron ran a stop sign in front of me and the folder Mick gave me to take to the station slid to the floor and the papers inside scattered everywhere.

"Great," I mumbled to myself as I found a spot in front of the station to park.

I pushed my body up and my legs out from under the wheel after I turned the car off and leaned over the seat, to get a better reach under the passenger seat, feeling for loose papers. I hoped these weren't in any particular order.

I thought I'd found everything and texted Tabitha, letting her know I'd be there in a few minutes. I got a thumbs-up emoji back.

I picked up the last stack of papers, thinking I'd have to explain this to Teddy or Nancy and I knew they'd think I was snooping. And for once, I wasn't. I know I could be bad about that, but I'd never do something like—

I was shoving papers back into the file when I saw Darrell and Lia's names, both in bold and highlighted in pink. I turned the interior light on in the car as the sun was setting to read more. I was searching around for my glasses when there was a knock on my window.

I jumped up and hit my head on the ceiling of the car.

"Sorry," Tabitha said, holding out both hands.

"I was just dropping this file off, then I was on my way to meet you at the park. Did you get my text just now?" I smiled up at her.

Tabitha stared at me, flabbergasted.

"You have no clue what I'm talking about, do you?" I asked, squinting my eyes.

Tabitha eyeballed me.

I held up the phone to show her the text and tilted my head, watching her carefully.

Tabitha's face contorted into different expressions of doubt, questions, and finally an uncanny glint hit her eye as an eyebrow lifted.

"I thought I'd lost my phone. Someone took it. Probably Janelle's killer," she said.

"They're waiting on me. Let me call Mick," I said, reaching for my phone.

"No! I'll handle this." Tabitha turned and dashed back to her car.

"Ooooh," I said to myself as my cell fell to the floor. I got out, leaving my tote and everything behind in my car, and sprinted after her. I yanked open the door and jumped into the passenger seat right as Tabitha hit the gas.

Chapter Fourteen

We were at the park in no time. Tabitha had been silent and looked deadly the few moments we were in the car. It was terrifying.

She sprung out of the car and I jumped to chase her but had no more than started to sprint when I clutched my stomach, fell to the ground, and puked.

Tabitha hesitated, looking around, then jogged back to me. "You stay here. Go back to the car. Here are the keys if you want to go for help."

Tabitha pushed the keys into my hands and sprinted off.

I started to get up and my stomach informed me that this was not an option. "No, I don't have time for this!" I yelled to no one.

I was panicking. Do I go get help or go after Tabitha? I didn't know what to do, so I ran after her while feeling for the keys she handed me. As I ran into the park, past the gazebo, toward the bench, I realized that there was pepper spray on the keyring. I pushed the lever to take the lock off. I also felt for the longest key of the bunch and pushed it in between my index and middle finger. I'd learned in a self-defense class it was a way to unexpectantly wound someone. They don't see it coming. It is a good defense method if someone is attacked while they are unarmed in a parking lot.

I slowed down again as I felt my stomach rumble. *No, not again*, I silently prayed.

I heard yelling that sounded like Tabitha, then a scream. My stomach lurched, but I managed to keep running as I spewed all over myself.

I finally arrived at the bench and found Tabitha straddling the bench, unconscious and bleeding from her head.

I looked around frantically, slapping at all of my pockets in search for my phone. *Crap, my phone's in my car and the killer stole Tabitha's phone!* I narrated in my head.

I shook Tabitha with trembling hands. "Tabitha, hey, it's Jolie. You're safe now. I'm feeling for a pulse, okay?"

She was sure to be confused and afraid when she woke up and given her hand-to-hand combat training, I did not want her mistaking me for her attacker. Thank goodness I felt a pulse. Weak, but there.

"Stay with me, Tabitha," I said loudly.

Tabitha moaned, reaching for her head and staggering to get up.

"No, just stay there. I'm thinking about what to do," I said, biting my nail. It was getting darker and I didn't want to leave Tabitha there, but I wasn't sure if she could walk back without help.

"I need to get him." She attempted to stand and fell back against the bench.

"Him? Are you sure? Did you see who it was?"

"I think—strong—experienced. Whoever it was, they've been trained. Rear headlock. They tried to choke me but—"

Keith appeared, dashing up to us in a panic. "Are you both okay?"

I filled him in and Tabitha pointed to the direction the killer ran. Keith threw something at me as he pulled his weapon and took off running.

I ran to what dropped a few feet in front of me. A cell. I called an ambulance.

"Did you see who it was, Tabitha?" I asked, seeing she was starting to go in and out of consciousness.

"No," she slurred, "...ski mask on."

"You said they tried to strangle you?" I asked.

Tabitha shook her head then stopped and held it, drawing in a sharp breath. "What's that smell?" Tabitha began waving her hand, trying to fend off the repulsive smell. "I can't—"

Oh no. I moved several steps away from her. I forgot I had thrown up while running. "That's, um, me."

Tabitha gave me a look of pure revulsion, leaned over, and got sick.

Chapter Fifteen

At the hospital, I saw that Lydia was back from her family vacation. She pulled me into a room and got some washcloths for me to wipe myself off and went to the lost and found and brought back a sweatshirt and some scrub pants.

"How was your trip?" I asked while changing.

"Obviously not as exciting as staying in good ole Leavensport, Ohio," Lydia said. "I saw Mick, Ava and Delilah going down the hall when I came in here. You want me to get them?"

"No, give me a minute. Do you have anything to settle my stomach?" I held it again.

"Yeah, I heard there's something going around," Lydia said, reaching into a cabinet.

"Things any better with your parents?" I asked.

"Things better with you and Chuck?" Lydia said flatly staring at me. She was referring to my biological father who she knew I had struggled with my entire life.

I put my hands up. "Okay, I won't ask."

"Let me run a few basic tests on you before you go. I'm going to give you some extra strength

Pepcid in the meantime." Lydia sat across from me and took a needle out of a sterile package. She wiped my arm. "This will pinch a little," she said as she slid the needle into my arm.

My body tightened slightly.

"Start with the Pepcid. We may have you take antibiotics depending on test results," she concluded.

I got up and grabbed my plastic bag full of smelly clothes and started down the hall.

"Try to eat bland foods until you hear back from me," Lydia yelled after me.

Yeah, right. I walked down the hallway to where I saw a crowd of people I recognized gathered in a waiting area.

Keith, Teddy, and Mick stood in a corner talking while Ava and Delilah waited in chairs. I saw Darrell walk toward the guys.

Keith glared at him. Darrell was his sister Denise's ex-husband who had tried to take the kids from Denise. Keith had moved his sister and kids in with him to help out.

Darrell said something to the group of men and Keith stormed off. I followed him.

"Hey, what's up? How's Tabitha?" I asked.

"She's going to be fine. They are keeping her overnight making sure it's not a concussion."

"What's Darrell doing back?" I realized Keith was more upset than normal because he and Tabitha were an item. I'd almost forgotten.

"He's getting the deal of a lifetime is what he's doing," Keith growled. "Coward ran. He got involved in some stuff I can't get into—"

I was going to scream if one more person told

me that there were things they couldn't tell me.

"—now, they are going to use him as an informant. So, he'll have no criminal charges filed. *Unlike* my sister."

"Wait, I saw that form. Is Lia an informant too? Do you know who Lia is—does Tabitha?" I pointed to Tabitha's room. People in town knew of Lia but not who she really was—Nestle's ex-wife in disguise.

"We do," he said, walking toward Tabitha's room.

Teddy had taken Darrell off with him and I walked back to where Mick stood. I noticed his phone buzzed, he looked at it, frowned, then put it back in his pocket. I got a bad feeling for some reason. Instinct or stomach bug?

Mick glanced up and saw me. He took two long strides toward me and pulled me to the side. "Are you okay?" He looked me over.

"Yes, I keep getting sick. I just saw Lydia and she ran some tests on me," I said. "She gave me some extra strength Pepcid to take until we find out more."

"You need to get home in bed and rest."

"You sound like Lydia. Rest, water, bland food. Fun!" I waved my hand.

"I just heard that Mary is getting out tomorrow," Mick said.

"What about Carlos?" I asked.

"We're still holding him for another twenty-four hours," Mick said.

I went to Tabitha's room to check on her, hearing Mick follow behind.

"I'm telling you, this person was trained in

combat and they knew what they were doing," she was telling Keith. "I maneuvered out of a head lock and they counter-axe kicked me in my head. Do you know how many times I tried that when working on my black belt? It was the one thing I never mastered."

I rudely interrupted. "Keith, how did you know to come looking for us?"

"I came out of the station, saw your car door open with your tote sitting there and knew something was wrong. I investigated and saw your phone and checked your text."

I really needed to learn to lock my cell.

"Wow, you're a pro," Tabitha said to Keith while smiling at me.

My attention span was off the charts right now. "Wait, hold on. A black belt in what?"

Tabitha grinned. "Krav Maga."

I stood very still. Mick looked at me, perplexed.

"Sorry, I'm feeling sick. I'm going to head home to bed." I kissed Mick and waved to Keith and Tabitha.

I knew exactly where I was going and it was not home.

Chapter Sixteen

I headed out of the hospital and ran into Ava.

"Where are you going in a hurry? Shouldn't you be resting?"

"If one more person tells me to rest—" I started.

"Calm down, princess!"

I filled Ava in on what happened and what I'd just realized and where I was going next.

"I'm coming with you," Ava said.

"UH-UH, no way!" I pointed to the interior of the hospital, turned on my heel and jogged to my car. I looked behind me and Ava was struggling to do a waddle-jog. I stopped, feeling sorry for her. She was already starting to show, which seemed early.

"Good Lord, I'm pregnant. Have a heart," she puffed, leaning on the hood of the Honda and breathing hard. She opened the passenger door, got in, and got a family-sized jar of chunky peanut butter from her new, big, mustard-yellow tote. She rooted around and pulled out a full-sized silver butter knife and a snack-sized bag of Cheetos.

"You aren't going to do what I think you're going to do, are you?" I took a deep breath. Did I take a Pepcid this morning? I did. My stomach churned and I swallowed the spit that formed in my mouth. "Oh Ava, please don't."

"I have to." Ava took the knife and slabbed some nutty peanut butter on a Cheeto and shoved it in her mouth, closing her eyes, then chewing and moaning.

I stared at her in disbelief and the smell changed from horrid to pleasant. I reached for a Cheeto, dipped it in the peanut butter and took a bite. Not bad.

"See, right?" Ava's eyes gleamed.

"It actually works," I said, starting the car and pulling out.

Five minutes later, I pulled into the Make Yourself at Home B&B and put the car into park. Ava popped another salty cheese delight in my mouth. I nodded in appreciation.

Ava looked at where I parked. "Why did you park all the way in the back?"

"Because we are going to take the back path." I pointed. "I want to catch the killer by surprise."

"It's dark. I think we're safe," Ava whined, not wanting to trek it.

"I told you not to come with me. Stay in the car. That way you can call someone if I'm not back in fifteen minutes."

I got out and started moving along the bushes toward the path that led to the gate of the pool where I knew a side door I could get into. Unfortunately, I'd been knocked out near here before and that's how I knew. I heard the voice of the person I was looking for talking on the phone outside and ducked behind a bush.

She was speaking in Italian and I couldn't translate, but I caught a glimpse of her face in the light by the pool. She looked angry, then she switched to English.

"No way! I don't want to come back now! No one knows anything. I need to stay here. I'm telling you I can turn him. He agreed to dinner with me."

I could make out an enraged expression on Imelda's face as she listened to whomever was on the other end of that call.

She raised her voice, "Wait just a minute! SHE found out about your little plan. I had no choice but to silence her—Fed or no Fed—"

She must have been cut off by her accomplice because she began to pace and kept looking as if she wanted to butt in but held her tongue. I moved a few steps closer as Imelda yelled out again, "No, the uh, the guy who has the cookie name—he purchased a plane ticket for me after I was already here. No one suspects a thing!"

NESTLE?!?

I felt a light tapping on my back and thought a branch was hitting me and reached back to swat it away and felt a hand.

I screamed out then slammed my hand around my mouth, eyes wide open. "AVA!" I whisper-yelled. "You scared the bejeezus out of me!" My heart raced and my breath came in gasps.

"What? I'm sorry. You keep running away from me," she pouted.

"I told you to stay in the car!" I scolded.

"It's creepy out there in the back of the lot by myself."

I rolled my eyes. "Stay behind me and keep your phone in your hand," I said, and handed my pepper spray to her.

"I think we should get licenses to have guns," Ava whispered at me.

I turned on my heel, staring at her in disbelief. "Ava, we can't even control where our puke goes. I don't think anyone would be safe if we had guns. That's a hard no!"

I turned back around and couldn't see Imelda anymore. I hoped she had gone inside. I had called and gotten her room number from my friend who worked here.

"Okay, let's go," I started quietly inching toward the gate. I could hear Ava crunching the leaves behind me.

"Shhh—" I turned to share my gesture with Ava and saw she was flat on the ground. "Ava," I started to run toward her when someone jumped out of a bush at me.

Imelda and I wrestled on the ground and I felt her long hair fall on my face as hands reached around my neck. I kneed Imelda in the stomach and she grunted, lifting me from the ground and jerking me around. She held me close to her body and I could see Ava lying on the ground as Imelda's muscular arms wrapped around my neck. She lifted my body slightly, allowing her to tighten her chokehold as she squeezed harder to cut off the blood from my head.

"You think you know Mick. You don't know him like I do. You don't know the things he's done," Imelda said as my eyes slid down to Ava and she became a blurred vision and I felt my body go limp, then everything went black.

Chapter Seventeen

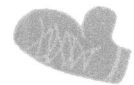

BEEP, BEEP, BEEP, BEEP.

"What the—" I lifted my arm groggily. My eyes opened slightly as I felt tubes attached to my skin and tried to pull them off.

"No, sweetie, don't do that." My mom stood over me on one side and Mick stood on the other side.

"Ava—" I choked out, trying to sit up.

Delilah appeared at the foot of the bed I was in. "Jolie, she's fine. Okay, just lie back."

"She's awake?" I heard my best friend ask anxiously.

"Ava?" I cried out. "The baby—"

"I'm here, girl," I swore I heard her choke up.

"She insisted the nurses move people around so you two could share a room and well, you know she gets what she wants." Mick grinned over at Ava.

I was getting my bearings and was able to look around.

"The baby's fine too," Ava said.

I looked at my mom, then at Ava questioningly.

"Mick and your family know now. They found out when we were brought in last night because Delilah blabbed it." Ava grunted at her wife.

"What? I had to tell the doctors you were pregnant!"

"I'm going to go get some coffee and let grandma and the family know you're awake." My mom rubbed my forearm and leaned over to kiss my forehead.

I was thankful for her interrupting those two.

Didn't matter the age, mom's kisses were the best comforts for a scared kid. I reached for her hand. "I love you, Mama."

My mom's pretty eyes filled with tears and she patted my hand. "My sunshine," she said, and took off quickly out of the room. I'm sure she was headed out to cry and thank God I was okay.

"So, why didn't Imelda finish us off?" I blurted out to no one in particular.

"I had come to while Imelda was choking you and reached out for the pepper spray you gave me and gave her a good full dose right in the face. She didn't see it coming!" Ava piped up, animating her spray finger and showing her superpowers. "She took off through the bushes and I called 9-1-1."

That left Mick, Delilah, and Ava over in the other bed, and a scraggily-looking man standing off in the corner behind the door. I thought I was imagining him and that maybe I was dreaming. I pointed and looked wildly at Mick.

"It's me, Jolie." A woman's voice came from the man.

I frowned in confusion.

"Lia," Ava said, like how could I not know.

My mouth fell open. "Lia!"

"Here, have some water." Delilah poured a glass of water into two cups filled with ice and added straws, handing one to me and one to Ava. She helped both of us sit up in bed as Mick went to shut the hospital room door.

Ava and I immediately gulped down our cups of water and Mick filled them both up again. I sat back carefully, placing my head on a pillow.

"What happened with Imelda?" I asked after getting the dry mouth under control.

"We caught her at the airport," Mick said. "It took three of us to take her down."

I didn't doubt that.

"We took her into the airport custody room and Teddy waited while the Italian police came for her. She's committed more crimes over there and they will make her pay and will work to get information from her. That worked for my family, too. I told them I heard she was picked up by the Italian police at the airport. They acted appalled as if Imelda wasn't capable of any of this behavior."

"Isn't your family suspicious that you think they are somehow connected to the criminal activities going on?" I asked.

"I'm sure they are. But they can't prove anything. Let me go back a bit," Mick started. "After you left the hospital so quickly last night, Tabitha kept telling Keith there was something weird about who she was fighting with earlier. She knew they had had combat training. She guessed based on the strength of the person and the height that it was a man, but she smelled perfume."

I nodded. "Right, your mother and sister told me about the extravagant perfume she wears."

"Next, she talked about Krav Maga and I remember you telling me Imelda trained in that. I put two and two together and realized you went after her."

"How did you know? I told you I was going home," I said.

"You get a look when something clicks," Mick said.

I gave Ava a look.

She nodded. "You really do. It's like a lion right before it attacks its prey."

That didn't feel like a compliment.

Lia stepped up. "Yeah, and I'm going to help out as best I can. Since I know what Jackson has done in the past and I've testified before, I'm going to try and find a way to get closer to him again and see if I can find out more information. Working at the shelter incognito will help with that. In a way, I'll be taking Janelle's place and I'll be able to deal with Nestle once and for all."

"We haven't figured all that out yet. There's no way we'll put a citizen in danger." Mick side-eyed Lia then looked over at me. "We found a broken crate at the shelter back in the woods where some olive oil had spilled out. Not enough to get him—as always. Also, there were things I knew that you didn't. I did NOT know Lia was Natalia, though."

"Okay, what about Bobby Zane, Asher, and Caleb?" I asked next attempting to change the subject while trying to take it all in.

"Bobby showed up to work like nothing happened. Said you didn't see what you thought you saw." Mick shrugged.

"What? Ask Betsy! She saw it too!" I exclaimed.

"I know," said Mick, "but he said they did

construction for him and he paid them then went with them to pick out the last of some lumber to finish up a project. By the time they got back, everyone was gone. He said he didn't think it'd be that long. We can't prosecute anyone if there is no crime and no one is reporting one."

"But we reported it!" I said.

"Bobby didn't corroborate it, Jolie!" Ava said.

"There's a lot to it all. Yesterday afternoon, Lia, Tabitha, me, Keith, Teddy, Harvey, and—" Mick started.

"Harvey?!?" Ava and I yelled in unison.

As if on cue, Harvey came into the room. "I was waitin' to hear my name."

Teddy walked in behind his dad and Keith squeezed into the ever-decreasing space with Darrell.

"So you didn't—" I said looking from Teddy to his father, Harvey.

"No, I'm not crooked. Although, it don't bother me none for people to talk. It actually helps." Harvey pulled at the waist of his pants and I noticed Teddy do so right after his dad.

"Where have you been all this time?" Ava asked.

"Mainly, I've been in Ireland. But I go to Canada from time to time. Big undercover operation that's been going on years, girls. Whoever is behind this has a family that's been in the game forever. But we know it's no big-named mafia. We narrowed that down here recently. The mob is the front."

"Geesh," I started. "That's pretty bal—"

"It is," Mick cut me off. "I'd love to say it makes

whoever is behind this dumb. But this dates back decades. They've gotten away with it for a long time."

"Everything leads back here," I said, looking around at all my loved ones.

"It's a pretty darn good place to hide," Ava said.

"Whoever's leading this thing, they are running it from here," Mick continued. "At least now they are. We're not sure if the operation started here or moved here, yet. There's something going on with Leavensport and Tri-City and politics are involved. I'm not sure it's happening at both ends yet but at different time periods we've been able to connect politicians, particularly mayors, to the organization."

I didn't think anyone else could fit in the room when Tabitha pushed the door open and walked in with Betsy and Carlos.

"Carlos!" I yelled and started to get up.

Teddy and Harvey brought Carlos to me quickly to keep me from getting up.

"Jolie, Ava, I can't even begin—" He choked up and hugged me hard.

"I'm so happy your name was cleared!" Ava said as Carlos moved around to hug her.

"Mary wants you both to know she is forever indebted to you for what you did for me and for Mirabelle while she was in the hospital."

"She's out?" I asked.

Carlos nodded. "This morning. She was there with Jorge, Mirabelle, and Spy when I got out." Tears began falling down his cheek.

"Wait, Betsy—" I looked from her to Teddy.

"I know everything," she said.

"So does Bradley," Delilah said.

Ava and I turned around to stare at Mick, wordlessly demanding answers.

"Our squad talked to Tabitha and the few other FBI agents who are involved yesterday. You and Ava have contributed a lot to the investigation and you did so with the help of Bradley, Lydia, Delilah, and Carlos. Everyone is invested in one way or another now. Some have training and badges, some have PI licenses, and others are merely townsfolk willing to play along to pass on information. No one is to say a word to anyone outside our group. Not your families, not Nancy at the station."

Ava and I grinned at each other. Who would tell Nancy anything?

"Not Baggy, Myrtle, Jenni—no one else. We will find ways to communicate, but moving forward, for the most part, we'll all be on the same page."

"What about Gemma and Peggy?" I asked, referring to our friends in the city who had helped us on multiple occasions.

"Yep," Mick said, "they are our eyes and ears in Tri-City for now. We're vetting someone to be undercover there with the mayor."

I took a breath. So, Lydia knew too? I wonder if that is why she was working to get along with her parents. Boy, I never would have seen all of this in high school. The old gang working undercover and some of us have to turn on our own families.

The door slammed into Harvey and he yelled, "WHAT THE FUTTOCK?"

I looked at him and laughed. "What?" I asked, seeing Lydia squeeze in with charts and glare at the number of people in the room.

"Futtock is the rib of a ship. Learned it in the Navy and me and the guys used to say in place of the bad F-bomb," Harvey laughed, patting Lydia on the back.

I had a fleeting thought about what Harvey just said about being in Ireland. That guy Liam was from Ireland. He mentioned a Chuck to Guido last winter. My biological father's name is Chuck and he used to leave for months on end, telling me he was visiting relatives in Ireland. He promised a thousand times to take me, but never cared enough to spend any time with me to actually do it.

Lydia interrupted my thoughts by saying curtly, "Okay, all of you need to leave. I need to speak to Jolie privately."

Betsy, Teddy, Harvey, Keith, Darrell, and Carlos all said their goodbyes and headed out of the room, leaving Delilah, Mick, me and Ava with Lydia.

I smiled at her then a fleeting thought occurred to me. If Maria was pretending to be on the phone with Imelda when I was with her and Mick's mom at Jeni's Diner, then that means those women knew what Imelda had done and that makes them complicit to Janelle's murder.

She eyeballed the three others in the room.

"I can't go anywhere!" Ava gestured at the bed.

"They can all stay whatever it is," I said shaking the thought away momentarily. "They're all family."

"Okay, well, looks like you don't have the stomach flu after all," Lydia said. "You've got what Ava's got, and it looks like the two of you are only weeks apart!" She hummed with a huge grin on her face.

"Are you serious?" Ava squealed.

"Really?" Mick's brown eyes danced, sparkled, and shined all at once as he looked down at me. He reached down to rub my stomach gently.

"Wait, is the baby okay?" I put my hands on my stomach protectively. I couldn't shake the last thing Imelda whispered to me before I blacked out. *You don't know him like I do. I know what he's done.*

"Well, the blood work showed your Beta-hCG levels are higher than normal. That means there's a strong chance that they are BOTH fine," Lydia said.

My mouth dropped open. I was excited and terrified all at once. One thing I knew for sure was that the Milano family would not come near these children. I had more reasons than ever to get to the bottom of all of this.

Recipes
Cast Iron Monkey Bread

**Recipe taken from:
https://www.melissassouthernstylekitchen.com/glazed-skillet-monkey-bread/

Ingredients

- 2 16.3 oz cans 8 count big refrigerated biscuits each biscuit quartered
- ½ cup butter melted
- ½ cup granulated sugar
- ½ cup light brown sugar
- 1 Tbsp ground cinnamon
- 1 tsp pumpkin pie spice or 1 tsp additional cinnamon
- ½ cup powdered sugar
- ¼ cup heavy cream, plus additional as needed to thin
- 1 tsp pure vanilla extract

Instructions

1. Preheat the oven to 375°F (temperatures may vary per oven). Butter the bottom and sides of a 12-inch cast iron skillet or similar. Set aside.
2. Separate biscuits and cut each into quarters. Roll each quarter into a ball. Dip in melted butter.
3. In a large plastic storage bag, mix together both sugars, cinnamon and pumpkin pie spice, if

using. Drop several pieces of dough at a time in the sugar mixture and shake until coated. Repeat until all dough has been used.
4. Place side by side in skillet. Sprinkle any remaining sugar evenly on top.
5. Bake for 30 minutes until golden and cooked through. Check at 20 minutes and lay a piece of aluminum foil on top if needed, to prevent over-browning.
6. Meanwhile, whisk together the powdered sugar, cream and vanilla until smooth. Drizzle over warm monkey bread. Serve immediately.

Gooey Texas Sheet Cake Skillet
**Recipe taken from:
https://www.thecookierookie.com/gooey-texas-sheet-cake-skillet/

Ingredients
- 8 ounces butter chopped (2 sticks)
- 1 cup water
- 4 Tbsp unsweetened cocoa powder
- 2 cups sugar
- 2 cups all-purpose flour
- 1 tsp baking soda
- 1/2 tsp salt
- 1/2 cup sour cream
- 2 eggs
- 1 tsp vanilla
- Frosting
- 6 Tbsp milk
- 3 Tbsp unsweetened cocoa powder
- 4 ounces butter chopped (1 stick)
- 3 3/4 cup powdered sugar
- 3/4 cup pecan bits

How to make the cake:
1. Preheat oven to 350°F and spray your 10-inch skillet with non-stick spray.
2. Combine water, cocoa powder, and butter in a saucepan. Bring mixture to a boil and then remove from heat.

3. In a large mixing bowl, combine flour, sugar, baking soda, and salt.
4. In another bowl, whisk the eggs, and then whisk in the sour cream and vanilla extract. Pour this mixture into the flour mixture, and stir to combine.
5. Now pour the warm chocolate mixture into the flour mixture, and whisk to fully combine everything.
6. Pour the chocolate cake mixture into the skillet, and bake for 30-35 minutes at 350°F.

   **NOTE: I like all my baked goods a bit on the gooey side. I have to play with times to get it where I like it.

How to make the frosting:

1. Combine milk, cocoa powder, and butter in a saucepan. Bring it to a boil.
2. Remove from heat and add in the powdered sugar. Use a hand mixer to beat until the frosting is fully smooth.
3. Use a spoon to gently stir in the pecan bits.
4. Pour the icing over the cake (still in the skillet) and give the cake about 10 minutes to cool before serving.

Top with scoops of ice cream, hand everyone a spoon, and have at it!

Cast Iron Frittata

**Recipe taken from:
https://www.countryliving.com/food-drinks/a32353869/cheesy-frittata-with-spring-greens-and-shallots/

Ingredients
- 12 large eggs, lightly beaten
- 1/2 c. heavy cream or crème fraîche
- 1/2 c. coarsely chopped fresh herbs (such as parsley, dill, and chives)
- 3 oz. mozzarella, shredded (about 3/4 cup), divided
- Kosher salt and freshly ground black pepper
- 2 tbsp. olive oil
- 1 tbsp. unsalted butter
- 1 shallots, thinly sliced
- 4 c. spring greens (such as spinach and turnip greens)
- 4 oz. plain or horseradish-flavored goat cheese, crumbled

Directions
1. Preheat the oven to 350°F with a rack in upper third. Whisk together eggs, cream, and herbs in a bowl. Add 1/2 cup mozzarella and stir to combine. Season with salt and pepper.
2. Heat oil and butter in a 10-inch nonstick oven-safe or cast-iron skillet over medium heat. Add shallots and cook, stirring occasionally, until soft, 2 to 3 minutes. Add greens and cook,

stirring occasionally, until wilted and liquid has evaporated, 4 to 6 minutes.

3. Increase heat to medium-high. Pour egg mixture into skillet; shake the pan to evenly distribute mixture. Stir once or twice, then cook without stirring until edges begin to just set, 4 to 6 minutes.
4. Sprinkle goat cheese and remaining 1/4 cup mozzarella over eggs. Transfer skillet to oven. Bake until golden brown and just set in center, 20 to 25 minutes. Let rest 5 minutes before serving.

Ravioli Appetizer Pops
****Recipe taken from:
https://www.tasteofhome.com/recipes/ravioli-appetizer-pops/

Ingredients
- 1/2 cup dry bread crumbs
- 2 teaspoons pepper
- 1-1/2 teaspoons dried oregano
- 1-1/2 teaspoons dried parsley flakes
- 1 teaspoon salt
- 1 teaspoon crushed red pepper flakes
- 1/3 cup all-purpose flour
- 2 large eggs, lightly beaten
- 1 package (9 ounces) refrigerated cheese ravioli
- Oil for frying
- Grated Parmesan cheese, optional
- 42 lollipop sticks
- Warm marinara sauce and prepared pesto

Directions
1. In a shallow bowl, mix bread crumbs and seasonings. Place flour and eggs in separate shallow bowls. Dip ravioli in flour to coat both sides; shake off excess. Dip in egg, then in crumb mixture, patting to help coating adhere.
2. In a large electric or cast-iron skillet, heat 1/2 in. of oil to 375°. Fry ravioli, a few at a time, until golden brown, 1-2 minutes on each side. Drain on paper towels. Immediately sprinkle

with cheese if desired. Carefully insert a lollipop stick into the back of each ravioli. Serve warm with marinara sauce and pesto.

Deep-Fried Cookies
**Recipe taken from:
https://www.tasteofhome.com/recipes/deep-fried-cookies/

Ingredients
- 18 (OR 1800—whatever amount works for you!) Oreo cookies
- Oil for deep-fat frying
- 1 cup biscuit/baking mix
- 1 large egg
- 1/2 cup 2% milk
- Confectioners' sugar

Directions
1. On each of eighteen 4-in. wooden skewers, thread one cookie, inserting pointed end of skewer into filling. Freeze until firm, about 1 hour.
2. In a deep cast-iron skillet or deep fryer, heat oil to 375°. Place biscuit mix in a shallow bowl. In another bowl, combine egg and milk; whisk into biscuit mix just until moistened.
3. Holding skewer, dip cookie into biscuit mixture to coat both sides; shake off excess.
4. Fry cookies, a few at a time, until golden brown, 1-2 minutes on each side. Drain on paper towels. Dust with confectioners' sugar before serving.

From the Author

Continuing to research universal topics that speak to all of us for this series is my absolute favorite thing EVER! That is what binds us all as writers and readers. The series themes consist of love/hate relationships with our family and friends, gentrification and urban sprawl, communities and individuals finding solutions for more tolerance in the world, and diversity. For *Monkey Bread Business*, I learned new information on the Prohibition and the nineteen twenties as well as some Krav Maga moves! Like I said in the last holiday book, *Yuletide Cast of the Iron Skillet*, history was never my best subject but I've been fascinated with studying the evolution of mafia and how they've changed and grown overtime. Agromafia is actually a thing and the Italian mafia has used some of their amazingly tasty olive oils to smuggle things other places!

Just like in *Yuletide Cast of the Iron Skillet*, another character was the real deal! Missy Smith has to be my biggest fan and I never in my life thought I'd say that. I mean, yeah, my mom is my biggest fan and so is my hubby. I'm just the okayest mom on Earth for my eight little heathen kitty cats, though. But to have a person who I don't know from Adam read my series and follow me on social media and send me gifts in the mail and chat with me—well, it's a dream come true. It makes me feel SO much more important than I actually am. So, Missy, thank you! I love you! I stalk you on social media, too! I may be YOUR number one fan-slash-stalker!

As always, if you find any mistakes in content, those are solely mine. If you'd like to share any with me, please email me at jrath@columbus.rr.com.

Pork Chopped to Death

You know what they say, you are what you eat, and Jolie and Ava are about to turn into everything they have been craving, including pounds of chocolate, pizza, pickles, and ice cream.

Mafia, urban sprawl, gentrification, newborn babies, and the lives of the Leavensport villagers will be altered forever. Change is inevitable. Jolie Tucker is a Type-A perfectionist with fanatic tendencies who detests the very thought of change. Regardless of what she wants, change is a comin' along with a grisly discovery of murder of one of the village's most beloved, mayhem between the villagers and the urbanites of Tri-City, and new dynamics of family dysfunction.

Get ready for a roller coaster ride from the peaks of new life, yummy food, and blossoming relationships to the lows of slayings, chaos, and war. The residents of Leavensport are in for the battle of their lives, and it's up to Jolie, Ava, and their crew to determine the future of their village.

Welcome to Leavensport, Ohio, where *DEATH* takes a *DELICIOUS* turn!

Read on for a Sneak Peek at a scene from Chapter One of Pork Chopped to Death which comes out July 23, 2021.

Scene from Chapter One

"Swollen ankles, dizziness, leg cramps, constipation, and my gums are so sore I want to scream." I tapped my stomach. "You better be worth all of this. I mean, you best be as cute as can be. I don't even want to know what the third trimester looks like."

I waddled over to the kitchen for a glass of milk and saw the jar of dill pickles and grabbed that too. Gulping two pickles in less than thirty seconds and chugging a huge glass of milk, I moaned with delight, rubbing my belly as my cell rang. I looked at the screen, then eyeballed the pickle jar again before answering.

"Hello?" I swished my hand around in the brine, in search of another green lump of deliciousness.

"Hey, I'm on my way over now," Ava's voice came from over the phone.

"Why, what's up?" I crunched.

"Something has happened to Mayor Nalini."

"What?" I put the pickle down, washed my briny hand, and rubbed Bobbi Jo's little head as she jumped up on the counter.

"He was shot."

About the Author

Moving into her second decade working in education, Jodi Rath has decided to begin a life of crime in her The Cast Iron Skillet Mystery Series. Her passion for both mysteries and education led her to combine the two to create her own business, called MYS ED, where she splits her time between working as an adjunct for Ohio teachers and creating mischief in her fictional writing. She currently resides in a small, cozy village in Ohio with her husband and her nine cats.

Other Books by this Author

Book One: *Pineapple Upside Down Murder*

Short Story 1.5 "Sweet Retreat"

Book Two: *Jalapeño Cheddar Cornbread Murder*

Book 2.5 A Holiday Novella *Turkey Basted to Death*

Book 3 *Blueberry Cobbler Blackmail*

Book 4 *Cast Iron Stake Through the Heart*—cowritten with Rebecca Grubb

Book 5 *Deep Dish Pizza Disaster*

Book 5.5 A Holiday Novella *Yuletide Cast of the Iron Skillet*

Links So We Can Stay Connected

Be sure to sign up for a monthly newsletter to get MORE of the Leavensport gang with free flash fiction, short stories, two-minute mysteries, cast-iron recipes, tips, and more. Subscribe to our monthly newsletter for a FREE Mystery A Month at http://eepurl.com/dIfXdb

Follow me on Facebook at https://www.facebook.com/authorjodirath

@jodirath is where you can find me on Twitter

www.jodirath.com

Upcoming Releases

Coming July 23, 2021, *Pork Chopped to Death*

Coming October 29, 2021, *Punkin Strudel Mayhem*

Look for a brand-new cozy series from Jodi Rath coming in 2022!

www.ingramcontent.com/pod-product-compliance
Lightning Source LLC
Chambersburg PA
CBHW030435010526
44118CB00011B/646